I0152755

CHURCH
CULTURE

WHAT MEMBERS DARE NOT SAY

Heavenly Realm
PUBLISHING

Heavenly Realm Publishing
Houston, Texas

Dr. Ethel Morale Gathers

Copyright © 2020 – Ethel Morale Gathers

All rights reserved. This book is protected by the copyright laws of the United States of America. This book may not be copied or reprinted for commercial gain or profit. The use of short quotations or occasional page copying for personal or group study is permitted and encouraged.

Published by Heavenly Realm Publishing,
PO Box 682532, Houston, TX 77268
1-866-216-0696

Unless otherwise identified, Scripture quotations are taken from the New American Standard Bible (NASB), Copyright © 1960, 1962, 1963, 1968, 1971, 1972, 1973, 1975, 1977, 1995 by The Lockman Foundation. Used by permission.

Scripture quotations marked KJV are taken from the Authorized King James Version of the Holy Bible, Copyright © 1982 by Thomas Nelson, Inc. Used by permission.

Scripture quotations marked NIV are taken from the New International Version Anglicized, Copyright © 1979, 1984, 2011 Biblica, formerly International Bible Society. Used by permission.

Scripture quotations marked AMP are taken from the Amplified® Bible, Copyright © 1954, 1958, 1962, 1964, 1965, 1987 by The Lockman Foundation. Used by permission.

Scripture quotations marked (MSG) are taken from The Message Version of the Bible. Copyright © 1993, 1994, 1995, 1996, 2000, 2001, 2002. Used by permission of NavPress Publishing Group.

Library of Congress Control Number: 2020915434

Interior Illustrations by: Little Giant Mfg. Co., unsplash.com; pexels.com; and shutterstock.com. Used by permission.

Editing by: Anita McLaurin, Joyce Robertson, Mary Wooldridge, and Heavenly Realm Publishing.

ISBN 13: 978-1-944383-20-6 (Paperback)
ISBN 13: 978-1-944383-21-3 (Hardback)

This book is available at: Barnes and Noble, Amazon, Books-a-Million, Borders, and at a store near you.

CHURCH
CULTURE

WHAT MEMBERS DARE NOT SAY

Dr. Ethel Morale Gathers

CONTENTS

ACKNOWLEDGEMENTS

I acknowledge first and foremost the memories of my late husband, Richard Alan Gathers, who always believed in me and encouraged me to move beyond my strength.

To our four daughters, Nathasha, Chastity, LeKeisha and Alaina, who constantly remind me of my strength and virtue, which comes from God. To Daryl and Michael for your respect and love. Thank you all for always believing in me.

To the memories of my late parents, John and Ida Sennett Morale, whose support was unfailing and love unending. To my siblings for your unwavering support. Thanks for the assurance that you're always there.

To ALL of my Pastors, including those who have gone before us, my spiritual parents in the faith. Thank you for the teachings and experiences I've gained in this walk of faith, without which this book would not be possible.

To my current Pastors of 30 years, Dr. LaSalle R. Vaughn and Co-Pastor Portia Brooks Vaughn, who awakened my eyes to the TORAH Studies and Feast Days of God, enabling me to become a better student of the Word.

To Pastors Victor and Sadie Alexander, who helped to enrich my spiritual growth with teachings of the Holy Spirit, and who always trusted me in the delivery of the Word.

ACKNOWLEDGEMENTS

To my nucleus of friends for your support and encouragement in writing this book. Thanks for believing in me.

FOREWORD

I first met Ethel Gathers in 1984 in Germany when she and her family attended our Gospel Church Services. I will never forget her quest for spiritual knowledge and understanding of God. "Why do we do this?" "What does that mean?" She wanted answers with proof, and explanations with evidence.

When Ethel taught a series of Bible Studies in the late 1980s, I realized, as her Pastor, that she had been a student of the Word for quite some time. The members of the congregation were often amazed and in awe because of her level of understanding and teaching of the Word. Yet, Ethel was so humble and gracious. Well learned, disciplined and very personable.

In her book, *Church Culture: What Members Dare Not Say,* Ethel presents ten chapters with subject matters that must be addressed in this present day. Questions are asked by members of the church today that must be carefully considered and answered. This book opened my understanding to truths about the church today, reminding me of my responsibility as a Pastor and leader.

This book is not just educational. It is pointed and powerful. It lit me up! Riveting, compelling, completely engrossing. I congratulate Ethel Gathers on this publication. I encourage you to read her book with open minds and hearts.

It is my hope and prayer that all who read it will be inspired to share it with other believers that we may continue to grow in the grace and knowledge of our Lord, Jesus Christ.

Victor & Sadie Alexander
Pastors and Founders
Heart of God Church Ministries, Inc.
Milton, Florida

Heavenly Realm

PUBLISHING

"Ethel is an outstanding author with a mission to win church structure from a Biblical stand-point. CHURCH CULTURE: WHAT MEMBERS DARE NOT SAY brings truth and accountability to the church and leadership with a two-edge sword. It is a great read with conviction of how the church should operate under the direction of the Holy Spirit."

INTRODUCTION

This is a non-fiction book based on my own personal experiences. The purpose of this book is to encourage those who struggle with "fitting in" as a Church member, and to bring awareness to those in positions of authority. Members hold discussions among themselves, but many dare not (or cannot) speak out on certain issues for fear of retaliation, demotion, or ostracism. We are encouraged to speak up for those who cannot speak for themselves, for the rights of all who are destitute; speak up and judge fairly (Pr. 31:8-9 NIV), which is the intent of this book. Having served at various levels within the Church from pew to pulpit, from member to leadership, this book contains personal testimonies of what I have witnessed "under the sun."

I grew up in the small rural town of Arnaudville, La. where the Church population was predominately Roman Catholic. My family were members of the local Catholic Church. It was here that my Christian foundation began. As a child, I can recall attending Saturday School, better known as Catechism. The Nuns (called Sisters) were our teachers. They taught us prayer memorizations and basic tenets of the Roman Catholic faith. Even today, I can recall some of the prayers: The Our Father, the Hail Mary, the Apostle's Creed, and the Act of Contrition. Services in the Roman Catholic Church were responsorial; the Priest led the readings and the Church responded according to the written words in the Missal. In the Catholic Church, I learned discipline and reverence for the House of God. The sanctuary was regarded as Holy. To eat, drink, chew gum and talk during services were forbidden practices. As children, if we attempted to whisper, the eyes of one of the "Sisters" (Nuns) would fall upon us and we knew we were being corrected.

9

After High School, I enlisted in the United States Air Force and proceeded to my first duty assignment following Basic Training. I lived in the dormitory and met many girls from different parts of the country and from various religious backgrounds. At the young age of 18, I began to "explore" different religions by attending services with my friends, Baptist and Methodist Church in particular. Likewise, they attended Catholic services with me. We alternated visiting each other's Church, as we were all from Church backgrounds. Although I didn't get entrenched in their church doctrine (as I was Catholic), I couldn't help but notice the differences in the order of service, or the "culture" of their Church.

The military afforded me many travel opportunities. While stationed in California I became acquainted with the Pentecostal Church, Church of God in Christ to be exact, at the invitation of a fellow co-worker. Here marked a pivotal point in my spiritual life as I became acquainted with Scripture memorization, which was highly encouraged. This of course sparked my interest, as it was new to me. My spiritual journey and quest for knowledge of the Word began, as I learned about salvation, having a relationship with God, and the Baptism and works of the Holy Spirit. Here I discovered a new Church climate and culture.

During my military career, my assignments overseas would bring me to the "Interdenominational" Churches, sometimes referred to as Non-denominational, Full Gospel or Gospel Service. The congregation consisted of members from various religious backgrounds. I'm thankful to God for this experience as well. There were no denominational churches around at the time; therefore, denominational doctrines were not the focal point. We studied and learned the Word of God together as *one*. In this book, my Church experiences are in Interdenominational Churches, unless otherwise noted.

I recently retired from civil service and found myself at home on lockdown, due to the coronavirus pandemic now plaguing the world. I had been seeking the Lord for guidance, doing some soul searching, and had many petitions before Him. One day while mopping my floors, the inspiration to write this book came to me so vividly. I put down my mop, got a paper and pen, and began to write. Within minutes, the title of this book along with the title of its 10 chapters was manifested, even in a pandemic! Therefore, I write of these experiences.

It is my desire that this book 1) draw attention to practices within the church not conducive to church growth and spiritual maturity, 2) offer solutions in accordance with the Word of God, and 3) address issues which *church members dare not say.*

It is my sincere hope that churches everywhere come together as *one* to glorify God's name. I invite you to journey with me. Let's go!

CHAPTER 1

Church Culture

A s an Environmental Science Instructor at the Academy of Health Sciences, Ft. Sam Houston, TX. during my military career, one of the courses I instructed was "Food Service Sanitation." As I reflected on course content, I saw a distinct similarity between the growth of microorganisms in food, and the growth of members in a Church. Just as climate and culture affect the growth of microorganisms, climate and culture also affect the growth of members in a Church. As a guest speaker at our local Church, the late Dr. Myles Monroe (Bahamas Faith Ministries) once said, "the Church is an organism; it breathes, it grows, it also excretes." While the comparison of the growth and culture of microorganisms to the growth and culture of the Church may be implausible to some, follow along as I make this abbreviated analogy. Abbreviated because I will describe in two short paragraphs, a lesson I taught in one hour!

1. Microorganisms (bacteria) are small in nature and require the use of a microscope to be seen. They take in food and water, reproduce, and give off waste products. Some may cause illness in a person who eats contaminated foods. Fortunately, all microorganisms are not harmful; some are friendly and serve a useful purpose (making cheese, butter, fermented milk, sauerkraut and vinegar). Some are useful in digestion of food. For microorganisms to grow they must have a suitable temperature. By regulating the temperature, the growth can be controlled. Most microorganisms causing foodborne illness will not grow in temperatures 50 degrees and below (cold), or 140 degrees and above (hot). Microorganisms causing foodborne disease grow best between the range of 68-113 degrees (lukewarm). They grow in the warmest of climates, become toxic, and is very dangerous to the consumer, causing illness and possibly death (Longree and Armbruster 6-17).

Jesus said to the Church at Laodicea:

> [15] *'I know your deeds, that you are neither cold nor hot; I wish that you were cold or hot.* [16] *So because you are lukewarm, and neither hot nor cold, I will spit you out of My mouth* (Rev 3:15-16).

2. When bacterial cells multiply under favorable conditions they pass through various phases, known as the growth curve (Longree and Armbruster 10-12).

    The **lag phase** - no multiplication occurs. It is possible for a decline to occur because some of the cells may fail to adjust to the new environment. There could also be "positive acceleration" during which the rate of multiplication is continuously increasing. If favorable, the lag phase is brief.

The **log phase** - Rapid growth occurs after they have adjusted to the environment. The number of bacteria increases, and the rate of cell increase is constant.

The **maximum stationary phase** - the increase and decrease cancel each other and thus the number of cells remain constant. The production of new microorganisms equals the death rate of old microorganisms.

The **death phase** - the number of viable cells decrease at a steady rate. Eventually all the cells of a culture die and become self-dissolving.

The worse phase for food is the **death** phase. However, unlike microorganisms with an end stage of death, Churches (organisms) can thrive forever if members adhere to the commands, laws and precepts of God.

Having served in the military 20 years, I was privileged to live in different states and countries and experience the cultural dynamics of various Churches. I found that as it is in the growth of microorganisms in food, so it is in the growth of membership in Churches. Churches have climates and cultures: some are hot, some are cold, some are lukewarm. While one Church may be conservative, silent, and still, another Church may be lively with lots of musical instruments and dancing. One Church may use hymnals, another may prefer to create its own unique style. I observed different Churches with different dress codes, some more strict than others. Church fellowships varied greatly in culture and administration. The bottom line is, as goes the culture so goes the people; people create culture. Considering the growth phases of microorganisms, I now draw a comparison to growth phases of a church:

Four Phases of Church Growth

As new members join the Church, they go through an adjustment period (**lag phase**). Unlike microorganisms, this process is not brief! They study the culture and doctrine of the church while trying to find their fit. Though they come with gifts and talents, most are reluctant to stepping out too soon. They are very observant of people and the order of service. Some may be babes in Christ, some may be mature saints, some may be broken and looking for relief or deliverance. Regardless of the level of growth in the Lord or status of the new member, it is vitally important that the current members show the love of Jesus and let that love mainstream the newcomer into the congregation. No need to brief them on personalities of others, who to befriend, and who not to befriend. They will find out in due time! Allow them to find their fit. Let the Holy Spirit do His perfect work! Simply love them into the Kingdom.

After the new member has adjusted to the Church (**log phase**), they should have an idea of 'where' they will be used in the Church. They'll find their own niche. Time, prayer and the Holy Spirit will direct them and more than likely they will remain. Rapid growth will occur, their gifts/talents will be used, and God will be glorified! Jesus appointed us to go out and bring forth fruit and said our fruit should remain (John 15:16).

The Church as a whole, or individual members, may enter a **stationary phase** where there is no growth. Churches sometimes appear to be at a standstill; they become stagnant. In the stationary phase, the increase and decrease cancel each other out and the number of cells (members) remain constant. Longree and Armbruster in *Quantity Food Sanitation* state, "The length of the stationary phase is strongly affected by the kind of organism, depletion of nutrients, and accumulation of waste products of cells. The reasons for the stationary phase are not completely understood" (11). Perhaps the reasons for fluctuation in membership is not completely understood because we fail to survey. Members come and members go. WHY? Is the Church stagnant in the Word? Is there fair treatment of members? Do members have an opportunity to grow? Are their gifts and talents being utilized? Does the *attitude* of 'complacency' exist? Does the Church lend itself to cultural differences? Sometimes Churches fail to grow because of the competition in the place! Can it be that the '**culture**' of the Church doesn't promote or encourage growth?

Competition among church members can certainly bring about the **death phase.** Learn to celebrate one another. Rejoice with those who rejoice, mourn with those who mourn. Let the strong bear the infirmity of the weak. Doing this will prevent the death phase of a Church. Treat one another fairly; God is no respecter of person. Love one another. The Apostle Paul said let no favoritism be among you, for God does not show favoritism (Romans 2:11). Competition, jealousy, envy, strife, and disrespect can cause the death of a Church.

In prison, the Apostle Paul recognized that some of his competitors were taking advantage of his imprisonment and preaching the gospel out of pretense. However, he wrote to the Church at Philippi stating:

> [14] .... *most of the brethren, trusting in the Lord because of my imprisonment, have far more courage to speak the word of God without fear.* [15] *Some, to be sure, are preaching Christ even from envy and strife, but some also from good will;* [16] *the latter do it out of love, knowing that I am appointed for the defense of the gospel;* [17] *the former proclaim Christ out of selfish ambition rather than from pure motives, thinking to cause me distress in my imprisonment.* [18] *What then?*

> *Only that in every way, whether in pretense or in truth,*
> *Christ is proclaimed; and in this I rejoice (Phil. 1:14-*
> *18).*

What an attitude! As long as Christ is proclaimed (preached), I will rejoice! Yes, I will rejoice! This attitude cancels out jealousy, envy, and strife and supports the work by others in the Body of Christ, the Church. It takes the Church totally out of the stationary and death phase, and promotes an atmosphere for God's blessings to flow, for in Unity, God commands His blessings (*Ps. 133:3*). If the Body of Christ would rejoice in the preaching of the Gospel by its members, regardless of church affiliation or denomination, this would certainly fertilize the ground for growth, and improve the climate and culture of the Church. The Apostle Paul said even if they are preaching out of selfish ambition, or even if they are trying to cause him distress, as long as Christ is preached, he will rejoice. Recognize that gifts and talents come from God. He places them in the Church for the edification and building up of the Church.

> *[11] And he gave some, apostles; and some, prophets;*
> *and some, evangelists; and some, teachers; [12] For the*
> *perfecting of the saints, for the work of the ministry, for*
> *the edifying of the body of Christ: [13] Till we all come*
> *in the unity of the faith, and of the knowledge of God,*
> *unto a perfect man, unto the measure of the stature of*
> *the fulness of Christ (Eph. 4:11-13 KJV).*

Scripture states that the Church must work to edify itself (in love) for the overall health of each member. Each member is commanded to engage in what leads to peace and to mutual edification (*Eph. 4:16*). This in itself promotes growth and enhances the **Culture of the Church.**

CHAPTER 2

Cliques in the Church

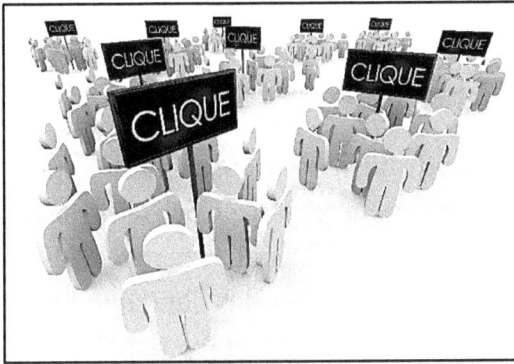

F rom Wikipedia, the free encyclopedia:

"A **clique** in the social sciences, is a group of individuals who interact with one another and share similar interests. Interacting with cliques is part of normative social development regardless of gender, ethnicity or popularity. Although cliques are most commonly studied during adolescence and middle childhood development, *they exist in all age groups* They are often bound together by shared social characteristics such as ethnicity and socioeconomic status.

Typically, people in a clique will not have a completely open friend group and can therefore "ban" members if they do something considered unacceptable, such as talking to someone disliked. Some cliques tend to isolate themselves as a group and view themselves as superior to others, which can be demonstrated through bullying and other antisocial behaviors."

Cliques, factions, divisions, groups, gangs, or whatever term one prefers, have always existed, and will continue to exist. People with similarities or common interests tend to gravitate one to another. Cliques have common behaviors, common identities, or group norms. Cliques are structured and may have roles assigned by leaders. According to Marianne-Webster, cliques are contentious or self-seeking ("clique").

As a student pursuing a degree in Counseling at St. Mary's University, the study of Groups was core to the Counseling curriculum. Groups exist everywhere, even in the Church, where relationships are formed. However, Christ never meant for the Church to be "divided." Christ is not divided. Problems exist when the norms/behaviors of cliques tend to diminish, disrespect, or undermine those excluded from the clique. Problems exist also when the clique is given advantages or privileges not extended to those outside the clique. Problems exist when "air of superiority" becomes the attitude of the clique and social rejection is experienced by members outside the clique. Problems exists when the clique is able to exert negative influence on those outside the clique. Actions are generally directed toward anyone the group perceives as a threat or source of conflict.

The Apostle Paul addresses this problem in the Corinthian Church. Paul calls the Church at Corinth to unity and brotherly love and reproves them for their divisions. He urges them to be joined together of the same mind, and to avoid divisions which alienates affection from each other:

[10] I appeal to you, brothers and sisters in the name of our Lord Jesus Christ, that all of you agree with one another in what you say and that there be no divisions among you, but that you be perfectly united in mind and thought. [11] My brothers and sisters, some from Chloe's household have informed me that there are quarrels among you. [12] What I mean is this: One of you says, "I follow Paul"; another, "I follow Apollos"; another, "I follow Cephas"; still another, "I follow Christ." [13] Is Christ divided? Was Paul crucified for you? Were you baptized in the name of Paul? (1 Cor. 1:10-13 NIV).

In this case, the cliques or factions were divided by **pride,** according to Matthew Henry Commentary, for they set their ministers at the head of their factions.

"They quarreled about their ministers. Paul and Apollos were both faithful ministers of Jesus Christ, and helpers of their faith and joy. But those who were disposed to be contentious broke into parties, and set their ministers at the head of their several factions: some cried up Paul, perhaps as the most sublime and spiritual teacher; others cried up Apollos, perhaps as the most eloquent speaker; some Cephas, or Peter, perhaps for the authority of his age, or because he was the apostle of the circumcision; and some were for none of them, but Christ only. So liable are the best things in the world to be corrupted, and the Gospel and its institutions, which are at perfect harmony with themselves and one another, to be made the engines of variance, discord, and contention" (Matthew Henry Commentary on 1 Corinthians 1).

[10] Where there is strife, there is pride, but wisdom is found in those who take advice. (Pr. 13:10 NIV)

The Apostle James says it this way:

What causes fights and quarrels among you? Don't they come from your desires that battle within you? (James 4:1 NIV).

Regardless of the reasons cliques exist, or who they choose as a leader, cliques that divide the Body of Christ or don't promote "oneness" in Him are altogether unhealthy to the Body of Christ.

Stages of Growth and Development

Cliques are normally studied during the adolescent period, the stage between childhood and adulthood. This age range varies anywhere between the ages of 12-20. Much research has been conducted on the subject of Adolescence and its varying stages. For the sake of this writing I'll concentrate on three which most therapist agree upon: early adolescence, late adolescence, and early adulthood. As the child moves from one stage to another, behavioral changes occur.

"In **early adolescence**, children seek independence and want more privileges and freedom from supervision so they can follow the dictates of a peer group. They try to be much like the others as possible. Later, they're concerned about status with immediate peers. They seek to be like one another and to conform to the norms of the group. The **late adolescent** shares the concerns of the early, but in addition he is concerned with ideas and values which may not match the cliques conservative code. He begins to set goals in respect to the entire world of independence and faces the chilling prospect of being on his own. In **early adulthood,** one moves toward greater independence, first car, first job, first apartment. However, psychologists hold that even while working, "they may not have yet achieved social and emotional independence" (Stone 420).

This quick review of the stages of adolescence leads to the question: what happens when the person reaches adulthood but have not yet achieved social and emotional independence? This condition makes it easy for "adult" cliques to form, as seen in organizations, schools, and the Church! Where social and emotional independence have not been achieved for whatever reason, adults will seek the approval or confirmation of others. They will seek validation of who they are. They will seek to belong, to conform to the group and to feel important. They will seek approval on decision making, as in the adolescence phase of growth and development. The writer of Hebrews addresses the "infant" stage of Christians who should have been more mature:

> "12 *For though by this time you ought to be teachers, you have need again for someone to teach you the elementary principles of the oracles of God, and you have come to need milk and not solid food.* 13 *For everyone who partakes only of milk is not accustomed to the word of righteousness, for he is an infant.* 14 *But solid food is for the mature, who because of practice have their senses trained to discern good and evil (Heb. 5:12-14).*

Apparently, the writer of Hebrews expected the audience to be more mature and to have more knowledge of Scripture than what they had. How do you gain knowledge of Scripture? By studying the Word.

Knowing God's WORD helps us to know TRUTH. Study of the Word must be done individually, not just corporately. Commit yourself to memorizing the Word in order to give an accurate account.

> [15] *Study to shew thyself approved unto God, a workman that needeth not to be ashamed, rightly dividing the word of truth (2 Tim. 2:15 KJV).*

On growing up spiritually, Matthew Henry states:

> Some persons, instead of going forward in Christian knowledge, forget the very first principles that they had learned long ago; and indeed, those that are not improving under the means of grace will be losing. It is a sin and shame for persons that are men for their age and standing in the Church to be children and babes in understanding. It is good to be babes in Christ, but not always to continue in that childish state; we should endeavor to pass the infant state. We should always remain in malice children, but in understanding we should grow up to a manly maturity (*Matthew Henry, Commentary on Hebrews 5).*

I have witnessed "under the sun," unhealthy cliques in the Church, with the end result of dissention, distrust, and disloyal behaviors. Unhealthy cliques are a hindrance to Church growth. Unhealthy cliques prevent healthy relationships and causes members to be disloyal one to another. Unhealthy cliques will mistreat members outside the clique just to gain the approval of their leader. Unhealthy cliques disrupt unity and must be dispelled from the Body of Christ in order for the Church to grow healthily.

Dispelling Unhealthy Cliques

To dispel unhealthy cliques in the Body of Christ, I offer the following:

- Treat others the way you want to be treated (Matt. 7:12).

- Avoid carrying the offenses of others. Jesus said we should bear one another's burdens, not offenses (Gal. 6:2).

- Strive for unity, not division; avoid belonging to unhealthy cliques and factions (1 Cor. 1:10).

- Respect one another (1 Pet. 2:17).

- Love one another as Christ loved us (John 13:34).

- Speak the truth in love (Eph. 4:15).

  Then will come about the saying of the Psalmist:

  "Behold how good and how pleasant it is for brothers to dwell together in unity (Ps. 133:1). SELAH (pause).

CHAPTER 3

Gift of Giving

*A feast is made for laughter, and wine maketh merry;
but money answereth all things (Eccles. 10:19 KJV).*

T his was Solomon in his quest to find the true meaning of life. He takes note of poor governments and he observes the behavior of pleasure-seeking Kings. The subject of "money" has always been controversial in the life of the Church. Nevertheless, it is necessary to operate a Church and to support causes that require financing.

Many people equate giving with money. While money is a necessary and valuable resource, there are many other ways to give besides money. When Moses was instructed to build the Tabernacle in the wilderness, God told him to tell the people (those of a willing heart) to bring resources of gold, iron, silver, bronze, fine linen, and other materials needed for the Tabernacle. God sent him Bezalel and Oholiab, *"and every skillful person in whom the Lord has put skill and understanding" (Ex. 36:1)* to assist. Recognize that your gifts and talents come from God, the giver of them all. Yes, we may acquire higher education and we may fine-tune skills in which we have interest; however, Scripture says *"all good and perfect gifts come from God" (James 1:17)*. Without His breath, passion and desire He placed within us, we would not be motivated to do anything. Without Him we could do nothing. Even time comes from God. Therefore, let us give back to Him the gifts and talents He has blessed us with, for the edification of His Kingdom.

While stationed in Germany from 1983-1988, I was a member of a small "Gospel Service" community where tithing was preached and practiced. The service was *ecumenical* in nature, with members from various religious backgrounds and we came together as one. The Chapel on Base loaned itself to Catholic, Protestant, and Korean Services. Attendees from any other denominational persuasion were generally grouped in the Gospel Service, a "catch-all" for all other religions.

To those unfamiliar with tithing, it is the practice of giving back to God 1/10th of your annual produce or earnings, formerly taken as a tax for the support of the Church and clergy. Merriam-Webster dictionary defines it as "an amount of money that a person gives to a Church, which is usually 1/10th of that person's income." Note that tithing was practiced in the Old Testament (Gen. 14:20; Num. 18:21-26; Mal. 3:10) and Jesus did not discourage it in the New Testament (Matt. 23:23). In our small congregation of approximately 150 members, monies received from tithes and offerings far exceeded the sum of the other three services. It was suggested to the Chief of Chaplains that the "Gospel Hour Service" be offered to reduce their giving, as this money would be turned in to the Morale, Welfare, and Recreation (MWR) fund at the end of the year. However, the Chaplain and Lay-Leaders determined NOT to suggest this change, as it is a

Biblical principle with associated blessings. In the end, the Chaplaincy Leadership determined that the monies be placed in a separate fund for use by members of the Gospel Hour Service, to attend conferences, retreats, and recreational tours. So, the church prospered spiritually, and naturally.

Granted, the example above is not indicative of the average Church today, as it was a military Chapel maintained by the Military. Most Churches today are either owned and funded by hierarchical religious organizations, or, independently started (the Interdenominational or Nondenominational Churches) and funded by the congregation's members. I am not on a finance committee of any church, nor do I represent any financial office affiliated with any Church. I have no access to any financial records of any Church. I simply write to relieve members of any misconceptions or "negative feelings" associated with the process of *giving*. Giving is to be done joyfully according to Scripture. The Apostle Paul puts it this way:

> *[6] Now this I say, he who sows sparingly will also reap sparingly, and he who sows bountifully will also reap bountifully. [7] Each one must do just as he has purposed in his heart, not grudgingly or under compulsion, for God loves a cheerful giver (2 Cor. 9:6-7).*

The Apostle Paul commended the Church at Corinth and at Achaia for their 'readiness' to give and their 'preparation' to give. He used them as an example to the Macedonian Church. One can conclude then, that giving is a matter of attitude. If you *want to* give, and you *prepare* (in advance) to give, then giving will not be done "grudgingly or forcibly." In fact, the Apostle Paul instructed the Church to prepare their givings in advance, so that the preaching of the Word would not be hindered upon his arrival. In other words, "I'm coming to preach the Word; don't hinder my time with your collections of offerings when I come."

> *1 Now concerning the collection for the saints, as I directed the churches of Galatia, so do you also. ² On the first day of every week each one of you is to put aside and save, as he may prosper, so that no collections be made when I come. ³ When I arrive, whomever you may approve, I will send them with letters to carry your gift to Jerusalem; ⁴ and if it is fitting for me to go also, they will go with me (1 Cor. 16:1-4).*

He stated, "…as he may prosper." In another occasion Paul stated, "…it is acceptable according to what one has, not according to what he does not have."

> *12 For if the willingness is there, the gift is acceptable according to what one has, not according to what he does not have. 13 Our desire is not that others might be relieved while you are hard pressed, but that there might be equality (2 Cor. 8:12-13 NIV).*

Giving grudgingly or forcibly happens when members give out of compulsion. They feel pressured to give, especially if they are in leadership positions or if they have "titles" in the Church. Gimmicks and propaganda may be tools used to either persuade or embarrass members who do not (or cannot) meet the Church's expectations. Open posting of one's givings in the hallways of the Church or on a flat screen visible to all, and announcements of one's givings, are tactics I have witnessed "under the sun." So much for giving in secret and allowing the Heavenly Father to reward openly! Oftentimes,

Churches go into debt under the guise of 'growing the ministry.' An indebted Church breeds indebted members. While one Church may suggest to its members to withdraw from their savings or investments to fulfill church obligations, another Church may suggest fundraisers such as bake sales, food trucks, outdoor events, bazaars, bingo games, church anniversaries, building fund anniversaries and special programs to pay off the Church's debts.

Prior to the Reformation period, the practice of selling indulgences was common. This is the practice of the (Catholic) Church accepting payments for the remission or mitigation of the severity of one's sin, which reduced the punishment one would receive by God for that sin after one's death (*Catholic Encyclopedia*). While it generated revenue for the Church, this practice was criticized by Martin Luther and was one of the causes of the Protestant Reformation. Reforms in the 20th century largely abolished the quantification of indulgences. Now, the modern-day Christian may say "we don't do that in our Church." Well, here are some rhetorical questions for consideration:

1. Do members who give more tithes/offerings get preferential treatment over those who don't?

2. Do members who give more have special privileges, are given more accolades, and are tolerated more?

3. Are the givers giving out of compulsion (pressure or coercion)?

4. Is marital discord problematic due to the pressures or disagreements over Church indebtedness or obligation?

5. Can one not provide for his household for the sake of meeting the needs of the Church?

I submit to you that if you answered YES to all (or most) of the above questions, we're no better than the Middle Age Church. I submit also that if you answered YES, the principles of giving according to Scripture are being violated. Giving is to be done from a willing heart and not out of compulsion. Giving is accepted according to what one has, not according to what one does not have. NOTE: there is no favoritism in God (Gal. 2:6). If your giving to the church causes you NOT to be able to meet the needs of your immediate household, you're worse than an infidel (non-believer):

> *But if anyone does not provide for his own, and especially for those of his household, he has denied the faith and is worse than an unbeliever (1 Tim. 5:8).*

When Ananias and his wife Sapphira sold property and brought some of the money to the Apostles and said, "this is ALL we received," Peter asked them "Didn't it belong to you before it was sold? And after it was sold, wasn't the money at your disposal?" In other words, it was yours to keep, so why would you give some and then lie to the Holy Ghost and say this is the entire amount? (Acts 5:1-4). Consequently, he and later his wife dropped dead after giving false reports of their giving and were buried according to Scripture (Acts 5:5, 10). Were they giving out of coercion or pressure? Were they giving just to be seen? Were they giving because they wanted to be counted among others who gave? Were they withholding due to greed? Regardless of the WHY they were giving, the Apostle told them "it was yours to keep." Let us examine the "WHY" as well as the "TRUTH" of our giving.

Jesus said, *"It is more of a blessing to give than to receive" (Acts 20:35).* There is joy in the act of giving when it is done with a pure motive. Your giving blesses the Church, it blesses others, it shows faithfulness to God, and in-turn it blesses you! So, let us give with the right attitude and give from a willing heart. Let us give out of LOVE, according to what we have. This is the type of giving that is acceptable by God.

> *For God so loved the world that He gave His only begotten Son, that whosoever believes in Him would not perish but have everlasting life (John 3:16).*

The Apostle Paul commended the Corinthians in their great works, but encouraged them to excel also in the gift of giving:

> *But just as you excel in everything, [and lead the way] in faith, in speech, in genuine and in your love for us, see that you excel in this gracious work [of giving] also (2 Cor. 8:7 AMP).*

When the wise men came to visit the young child (Jesus) in Bethlehem of Judaea, they didn't come empty-handed, they came *prepared* to give. They gave gifts of gold, frankincense, and myrrh (Matt. 2:11). When the Queen of Sheba came to visit Solomon, she didn't come empty-handed, she came *prepared* to give. She gave an abundance of spices, gold, precious stones (1 Ki. 10:10). God instructed the Israelite *men*, when they come before Him during the three feast days (the Festival of Unleavened Bread, the Festival of Harvest, and the Festival of Tabernacles), not to come before Him empty-handed, come *prepared* to give (Deut. 16:16). Boaz blessed Ruth with six measures of barley as she *prepared* to return to her mother-in-law

33

(Naomi) and told her, "Don't go to your mother-in-law empty-handed" (Ru. 3:17).

Therefore, let us learn from the examples set before us by coming "*prepared* to give" out of what we have when we come to the House of God. This in itself eliminates giving compulsively and grudgingly, for God loves a cheerful giver. Let us do as the Apostle Paul suggested and excel in this gracious gift: the gift of giving. For it is more of a blessing to give than to receive.

CHAPTER 4

Pulpit Bullying

Wikipedia Encyclopedia: **Bullying** *is the use of force, coercion, or threat, to abuse, aggressively dominate or intimidate. The behavior is often repeated and habitual. One essential prerequisite is the perception (by the bully or by others) of an imbalance of physical or social power. This imbalance distinguishes bullying from conflict. Bullying is a subcategory of aggressive behavior characterized by the following three minimum criteria: (1) hostile intent, (2) imbalance of power, and (3) repetition over a period of time. Bullying is the activity of repeated, aggressive behavior intended to hurt another individual, physically, mentally, or emotionally ("bullying").*

W e've heard of bullying on the school campuses, bullying on jobs by supervisors or upper level management, bullying in politics, bullying in relationships, even cyber bullying. Suicides and attempts at suicide have been committed due to pressures stemming from bullying. Having been a member of several churches during my military career and having witnessed firsthand the varying behaviors in the pulpit across denominational lines, I have witnessed "under the sun" a behavior which I will now refer to as **pulpit bullying!** Yes, bullying can come directly from the pulpit, where the old adage "there's power in the mic" holds true. Some speakers feel empowered to use their words as a painful weapon, knowing there's no recourse for rebuttal. Aggressive behaviors are intended to hurt another individual, physically, mentally, or emotionally, which is the stated definition of bullying. When the pulpit becomes a place for bullying or attacking others, venting out personal frustrations, demonstrating power plays stemming from insecurities, and expressing open anger, the integrity of the speaker has been breached. The purpose of the pulpit is to teach, guide, encourage, preach the Word of God, and win souls to Christ. Anything short of this, the clergy have failed the pulpit. SELAH (pause).

I traveled to Kansas, City, Mo. in March 2020 to be with my older brother, age 80, whose health was quickly declining. While there, the hospital went on lockdown due to the coronavirus pandemic. The hospital allowed me to room with my brother, due to his placement on hospice care status. During this three-week hospital stay, I prayed and meditated a lot. I had many intimate conversations with God, as I sought Him fervently. The world was in chaos! While the medical professionals sought to find answers to this pandemic, I sought to find answers from God. I prayed and sought the Lord for healing, and instructions on how to effectively pray for my brother. While waiting patiently, I was blessed to hear a message by Dr. Tony Evans entitled, "Divine Disruption." He spoke from 2 Chron. Chapter 15, which tells of chaos in the land of Israel due to 1) There was no God, 2) There was a void of teaching Priests, and 3) There was no law. He spoke of "**when pulpits fail**," identifying causes such as man's standards being preached rather than God's standards, and 'uncertain sounds' coming from the pulpit. He said pulpits should return to speaking to the **culture** of God's Word rather than the culture of the Church. Dr. Evans addressed the misuse of pulpits and admonished those with pulpit access to return to the heart of God and preach messages that draw people back into *relationship* with God. He stated the purpose of the pulpit is to push God's agenda, not man's, and to prompt people to surrender their lives to the Lord and be saved (Dr. Tony Evans, message: *Divine Disruption,* YouTube, 22 March 2020).

Well, I don't know if this message touched your heart or not, but it was truly an answer to several of my prayers as I cried to God for understanding and guidance. The misuse of pulpits distracts members and hinders the work and benefits of the Holy Spirit. The Word of God saves. The Word of God heals. The Word of God delivers. The Word of God comforts. The Word of God draws. The Word of God discerns. Preach the Word and allow it to do its perfect work!

> *For **the word of God** is quick, and powerful, and sharper than any two-edged sword, piercing even to the dividing asunder of soul and spirit, and of the joints and marrow, and is a discerner of the thoughts and intents of the heart (Heb. 4:12 KJV).*

When the Word of God is not the main message from the pulpit, the spiritual growth of its members is stunted, and they remain in an infantile state. Members grow to become giant infants. In the words of the Apostle Paul, they should be teaching others but still have need of others to teach them the elementary principles of the Word. They have need of milk and not solid foods. For everyone that uses milk is unskillful in the Word of righteousness, for he is a babe (Heb. 5:12-13). As infants we should desire the sincere milk of the Word, yes, but in time we should be desiring meat. When Jesus stood in the pulpit, He preached the Word, quoting from the Prophet Isaiah (Luke 4:16-30).

In the Catholic Church where I grew up until the age of 18, the structure was more authoritative in nature. Only the Priest brought the Word, normally in a near monotone voice without inflections, (unless he was angry about a matter). However, whatever he said was considered the authoritative Word and no one questioned it. We could "take it to the bank." It was law and it was the unadulterated Word that no one challenged. The pulpit was a place from which the authoritative Word of God flowed, and the Church sanctuary was a place of reverence. One dare not walk, talk or look around during the exposition of the Word. In fact, a holy hush was the standard.

I later witnessed in the Pentecostal Church the pulpit to be a place encouraging participation from the congregation. Scripture memorization and responding with Scripture and "Amen" was the norm. In fact, the more energetic the congregation responded, the more energetic the Preacher became and vice-versa. The Preacher thrived on the energy of the congregation. It was easier to preach to an active crowd than one that passively listened. The study of Scripture was foremost, with use of occasional competitive activities in the form of Bible drills to promote knowledge of Scripture. The Apostle Paul also encouraged this:

> *Study to show yourself approved unto God, a Workman needeth not be ashamed, rightly dividing the Word of Truth (1 Tim. 2:15 KJV).*

The "Pastor" or "Reverend" was the authoritative figure and addressed the congregation in general. My experience was such that the older women called "Mothers" were the authority over the women of the Church and engaged in teaching and correcting the women as needed (Titus 2:3-5). The role of the Mothers sort of reminded me of the Nuns in the Catholic Church, their looks spoke volumes! There was strength in their looks; however, we sensed their love, even in a rebuke!

Open Rebukes

Pulpit bullying is not to be confused with open rebukes and corrections, which is permitted by Scripture. The Apostle Paul said Scripture is good for teaching, correcting, rebuking, and instructing in righteousness (2 Tim. 3:16). He instructed Timothy to rebuke "them that sin" before all, so that others may fear (1 Tim. 5:20). Throughout Scripture we see examples of corrections and rebukes:

1. Paul corrected Peter for being hypocritical. Peter had been visiting and eating with the Gentles; however, when James and those of the circumcision appeared, Peter removed himself from the Gentiles, causing others to be led astray (Gal. 2:11-13).

2. Samuel rebuked Saul for his disobedience. Saul was instructed to wait for Samuel before offering the sacrifice. Saul became impatient and offered the sacrifice before Samuel arrived (1 Sam. 13:11-15).

3. Jesus rebuked Peter saying he had man's interest in mind and not God's interest (Matt. 16:23).

4. Jesus rebuked Satan with Scripture for his attempts to make Him sin (Matt. 4:3-11).

5. Jesus rebuked the money changers for turning His Father's house into a den of thieves (Matt. 21:13).

The list goes on and on. However, the above cited examples did not occur in a pulpit. Scripture doesn't specify *"where"* rebukes and corrections should take place, but it does specify *"why."*

> [16] *All Scripture is inspired by God and profitable for teaching, for reproof, for training in righteousness;* [17] *so that the man of God may be adequate, equipped for every good work (2 Tim. 3:16, 17).*

> *All Scripture is God-breathed [given by divine inspiration] and is for instruction, for conviction [of sin], for correction [of error and restoration to obedience], for training in righteousness [learning to live in conformity to God's will, both publicly and privately—behaving honorably with personal integrity and moral courage];* [17] *so that the man of God may be complete and proficient, outfitted and thoroughly equipped for every good work (2 Tim. 3:16, 17 AMP).*

Therefore the *"why"* is to "polish up" the people of God, so that they may be adequate, equipped for every good work, complete and proficient. Rebuking and reproofing should not be for the purpose of intentionally hurting another individual, physically, mentally, or emotionally (that is bullying, by definition), but to equip them for good works. In fact, *"an open rebuke is better than love that is concealed, and as iron sharpens iron so one person sharpens another" (Pr. 27:5, 17).* We are encouraged to be skilled and sharpened in the Word.

In his book, *The Art of Communicating*, Zen Master Thich Nhat Hahn speaks of communication as essential food. Hahn states, "Effective communication is as important to our well-being and happiness as the food we put in our bodies. It can be either healthy and nourishing, or toxic and destructive" (Hahn 1). The following is an excerpt:

> "When we say something that nourishes us and uplifts the people around us, we are feeding love and compassion. When we speak and act in a way that causes tension and anger, we are nourishing violence and suffering. We often ingest toxic communication from those around us and from what we watch and read. Are we ingesting things that grow our understanding and compassion? If so, that's good food. Often, we ingest communication that makes us feel bad and insecure about ourselves OR judgmental and superior to others. We can think about our communication in terms of nourishment and consumption." (A best-selling author, Hahn has authored books as *Helps to Be Reminded of How We Use Words; Peace in Every Step; True Love; Silence; Loving Speech,* and others).

What is **your** pulpit diet? Are you nourished and uplifted after a meal? Are you eating foods which cause tension and anger? Are you eating toxic communication? Are you ingesting things which grow your understanding and compassion? What type of food is going into your spiritual body? According to Hahn, effective communication can be either healthy and nourishing, or it can be toxic and destructive. The pulpit is not the place for spitting out venomous words to intentionally tear down. Examine your diet. The sanctuary should be a place of healing, a place of refuge, and an atmosphere for drawing closer to God. His **house should be a place to** rekindle a relationship with Him, **gain** guidance and retrospect like the Psalmist did:

41

(Psalm 73:1-3, 16-17, 21-24)

Surely God is good to Israel,
To those who are pure in heart!
² But as for me, my feet came close to stumbling,
My steps had almost slipped.
*³ For I was **envious** of the arrogant*
As I saw the prosperity of the wicked.
When I pondered to understand this,
*It was **troublesome** in my sight*
¹⁷ Until I came into the sanctuary of God;
Then I perceived their end.
*When my heart was **embittered***
*And I was **pierced** within,*
*²² Then I was **senseless** and **ignorant;***
*I was like **a beast** before You.*
²³ Nevertheless I am continually with You;
You have taken hold of my right hand.
²⁴ With Your counsel You will guide me,
And afterward receive me to glory.

Before coming into the sanctuary, the Psalmist describes his feelings of envy, bitterness, hurt, senseless, ignorance, and being without substance (to name a few). Have you ever entered the sanctuary feeling broken, betrayed, lonely, disappointed, angry, sick, tired, or confused? You name it. Did you not come to the sanctuary to hear a "Word from the Lord?" You hoped to be uplifted, you yearned for relief, you hoped to return home in a better state from which you came. How did it feel to return home the same way you entered the sanctuary, or worse?

Matthew Henry Commentary describes the Psalmist's sanctuary encounter:

> *From all this arose a strong temptation to cast off religion. He prayed to God to make this matter plain to him; then he understood the wretched end of wicked people; even in the height of their prosperity they were but ripening for ruin. The sanctuary must be the resort of a tempted soul (Ps. 73).*

Throughout the Book of Proverbs, we see the effects of harsh and rash words. Just to name a few:

> *There is one who speaks rashly like the thrusts of a sword, but the tongue of the wise brings healing (Pr. 12:18).*

> *A gentle answer turns away wrath, but a harsh word stirs up anger (Pr. 15:1).*

> *A soothing tongue is a tree of life, but perversion in it crushes the spirit (Pr.15:4).*

Effective Communication

Some may remember in their formal education training, the three components of communication as the sender, the message and the receiver. If the sender was not clear in its delivery, the message became distorted and resulted in the receiver getting a mixed or distorted message. The communication process reached its final point when the message had been successfully transmitted, received, and understood. This model has since then been extended to 5 elements of effective communication, to include 1) sender and receiver, 2) medium that carries the message, 3) contextual factors, 4) the message itself, and 5) feedback (Mastery Technologies, Inc., 2020).

This process incorporates such factors as cultural differences, use of language, individual perceptions, attitudes, tone, volume, and personalities. People often mistake volume, passion, and excitement for the "anointing." When did yelling and screaming and humming the Word become the anointing? When did targeting or striking at church members (due to something the speaker was displeased about) become the anointing? The speaker's tone, method of delivery, emotional status, and unresolved personal or church issues, can hinder the anointing and impact the intent of the message. Leaders/speakers must submit themselves and ALL of their unresolved issues to God and seek His face before attempting to minister to God's people. It is then, and only then, that the anointing will follow.

The anointing requires no assistance. Just as the Word of God is swift, powerful, sharp, it pierces, divides and discerns (Heb. 4:12), so does the anointing; it flows with the Word. To the speaker charged with delivering the Word to its congregants, please consider these factors that affect communication and let them not become 'barriers' to effective communication. If the message is not received and understood, communication is not effective. Consider the congregants as "sheep of God's pasture" and that you are charged with feeding the sheep. Focus on drawing people to Christ; recall the mission as described by our Lord and Savior, Jesus Christ:

> [18] "THE SPIRIT OF THE LORD IS UPON ME, BECAUSE HE
> ANOINTED ME TO PREACH THE GOSPEL TO THE POOR. HE
> HAS SENT ME TO PROCLAIM RELEASE TO THE CAPTIVES, AND
> RECOVERY OF SIGHT TO THE BLIND, TO SET FREE THOSE WHO

ARE OPPRESSED,

[19] TO PROCLAIM THE FAVORABLE YEAR OF THE LORD"

(Luke 4:18-19).

To the congregant, understand that speakers are human and perhaps share the same issues/difficulties as you do. Pray for us, that God may use us to fulfill His purpose, that men may return to Him in true repentance and serve the living God. May the hearers of the Word, like the Psalmist who went to the sanctuary for relief, always remember that those who seek Him, find Him!

CHAPTER 5

Open Door Policy

I n the military some Commanders have what is known as an "open door policy." This doesn't mean that anyone may walk into their office at any time without an appointment. Rather, it means the Commander would avail him/herself at the request of a service member to discuss any matter deemed important. I observed this policy to be practiced in corporate America as well.

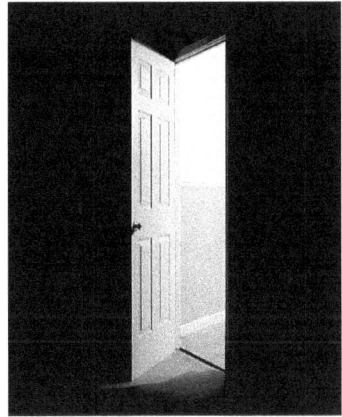

During my various assignments, I had the privilege of belonging to small Churches (less than 100 members) as well as mid-size Churches (100-400 members). I've never been a member of a mega Church with membership in the thousands. I have observed this open-door policy operates more in smaller Churches, whereby the Pastors, Parishioners, and Lay-Leaders were closer connected to the members. It was not uncommon for Leaders to fellowship with members, to go on social outings, to be invited into the member's homes and vice-versa. It was not uncommon for Leaders to do hospital visits and make home and convalescent visits to the sick or those with special challenges. It was not uncommon for Leaders to place a phone call to a member who may have missed service that day. A "just because" call would be made to check on their wellbeing. The community was closer-knit in the smaller Churches.

However, in mid-size Churches, less of an open-door policy existed and the practice of "delegation of authority" was more prevalent. Understandably so, the greater the membership, the greater the need for expansion of Leadership. The military term "span of control" can easily be violated when one person attempts to carry a load too great or supervise an audience beyond their control. This can easily be seen in the book of Exodus as Moses tried to counsel the entire Nation of Israel alone. He was corrected by his Father-in-law, Jethro:

> [13] *The next day Moses took his seat to serve as judge for the people, and they stood around him from morning till evening.* [14] *When his father-in-law saw all that Moses was doing for the people, he said, "What is this you are doing for the people? Why do you alone sit as judge, while all these people stand around you from morning till evening?"* [15] *Moses answered him, "Because the people come to me to seek God's will.* [16] *Whenever they have a dispute, it is brought to me, and I decide between the parties and inform them of God's decrees and instructions."* [17] *Moses' father-in-law replied, "What you are doing is not good.* [18] *You and these people who come to you will only wear yourselves out. The work is too heavy for you; you cannot handle it alone.* [19] *Listen now to me and I will give you some advice, and may God be with you. You must be the people's representative before God and bring their disputes to him.* [20] *Teach them his decrees and instructions, and show them the way they are to live and how they are to behave.* [21] *But select capable*

men from all the people—men who fear God, trustworthy men who hate dishonest gain—and appoint them as officials over thousands, hundreds, fifties and tens. [22] Have them serve as judges for the people at all times, but have them bring every difficult case to you; the simple cases they can decide themselves. That will make your load lighter, because they will share it with you. [23] If you do this and God so commands, you will be able to stand the strain, and all these people will go home satisfied." [24] Moses listened to his father-in-law and did everything he said. [25] He chose capable men from all Israel and made them leaders of the people, officials over thousands, hundreds, fifties and tens. [26] They served as judges for the people at all times. The difficult cases they brought to Moses, but the simple ones they decided themselves. [27] Then Moses sent his father-in-law on his way, and Jethro returned to his own country (Ex. 18:13-27 NIV).

Delegation of authority relieves the Leader of burdensome tasks and administration, as in the case with Moses. It also helps to organize people into auxiliaries or smaller groups. Church Leaders and members oftentimes experience burnout from attempting to do more than they can effectively manage.

I had the privilege of conducting interviews with Church members of larger and mega churches (names held confidentially). When asked "do you ever speak with your Pastor?" Most said, "No" or "never." I asked if they were able to speak with their Pastor if there was a serious problem or emergency. Most said "No" or "Absolutely not." They explained that they were assigned Elders or Lay-Leaders according to their geographic location. One explained, "Some people are close to them, those in the inner circle, all others are directed to the Elders, Church Counselors, or Lay-Leaders."

A problem exists, however, when Leaders are "able" to practice the open-door policy but choose not to. Members often voice or complain that "the Pastors are untouchable." They are disappointed about not hearing personally from their Pastors when they are sick, or when they have lost a loved one. They complain of not getting a phone call. Pastors in this category tend to delegate and possibly view this as an Elder's, Associate Pastor's, or someone else's responsibility. However, members in general want to and need to hear directly from their Pastors. The absence of this connection may translate to some members as an attitude of apathy on the Pastor's or Leader's part. The message perceived may also convey a feeling of being non-important to their leaders.

When the donkeys of Saul's father (Kish) were lost, he sent Saul to look for them:

> *Now the donkeys of Kish, Saul's father, were lost. So,*
> *Kish said to his son Saul, "Take now with you one of*
> *the servants, and arise, go search for the donkeys"*
> *(1 Sam. 9:3).*

Growing up on a farm in the Southwestern part of Louisiana, I can recall when occasionally a farm animal (cow, horse, mule) would manage to escape the pastureland. My father and brothers would go looking for them, find them and bring them back! The lost animal was as important to my Dad as the lost donkey was to Saul's father. In Biblical days, the occupation of Shepherds and Farmers was dominant. If the animals were that important to the owners that they would go out to find them, how much more should we value the souls of men? The parable of the lost sheep (Luke 15:4) shows that each person is precious and important to God, so He goes after us and finds us! Christ came to seek and to save the lost (Luke 19:10). Let us search our own hearts and move with compassion to reach the lost or those in need.

> *Seeing the people, He felt compassion for them, because they were distressed and dispirited like sheep without a shepherd (Matt. 9:36).*

Jesus also wept at the tomb of Lazarus because he was moved with compassion (John 11:33-35). He wept because the ones he loved were weeping. The Apostle Paul said, *"Rejoice with those who rejoice, mourn with those who mourn" (Rom. 12:15).*

The open-door policy is a method of showing compassion. Just as Commanders take time to listen to the servicemen's issues and offer assistance and guidance, how much more should we in the Body of Christ offer the same one to another? In the absence of an open-door policy, can we show compassion as Jesus did? Can we take time to hear or listen to the concerns of others in the Body of Christ and not turn a deaf ear? Can we visit them in the hospitals, nursing facilities and convalescence homes? If we are unable to visit, can we at least call and let them know we care? Can we offer rides to those in need? Can we rejoice when others rejoice? The time is long overdue for compassion to return to the Body of Christ. In the absence of "open-door policies," let us open up the doors of our hearts and take time to listen to one another.

In large or mega churches where duties are delegated due to the vast number of members, may we never become so untouchable that members feel there is no connection with the Pastor or with Leadership. The practice of "leadership distancing" is one that goes against the grain of fellowship and against the concept of availability. A Church will never be a "Great House" without compassion one for another. Let us pray that God will turn our HEARTS into an open door, that love and compassion will return to the Body of Christ.

CHAPTER 6

Feeding the Flock

Pay careful attention to yourselves and to all the flock, in which the Holy Spirit has made you overseers, to care for the church of God, which he obtained with his own blood (Acts 20:28).

The Apostle Paul instructs Church Leaders to first pay attention to their own lives. He reminds them of the charge by the Holy Spirit to care for the Church of God. He also reminds them that Jesus purchased it (the Church) with His own blood. Therefore, Paul admonishes the leaders to "care for" the flock (love them, feed them, lead them, teach them, be an example to them) because they serve as overseers, appointed by the Holy Spirit.

Notice the Scripture says to pay careful attention to *ALL* the flock. It was never Jesus' intention that any of the flock be excluded or left behind. It is the duty of Shepherds to care for *ALL* the flock. Even if one goes astray, Jesus says A good Shepherd will leave the ninety-nine and go after the one that went astray (Matt. 18:12–14; Luke 15:3–7). This may not always be an easy task for Shepherds. Moses' task was not easy. An easy task would be to "care for the ones you love" or "care for the ones who are easy to shepherd." However, that is not the command! Shepherds are not at liberty to pick and choose 'which' of the flock they will care for. They are not at liberty to pick and choose which of the flock warrants their prayers. On the contrary, Jesus said:

> *[27]But I say to you who hear, love your enemies, do good to those who hate you, [28] bless those who curse you, pray for those who mistreat you. [29] Whoever hits you on the cheek, offer him the other also; and whoever takes away your coat, do not withhold your shirt from him either. [30] Give to everyone who asks of you, and whoever takes away what is yours, do not demand it back. [31]Treat others the same way you want them to treat you. [32] If you love those who love you, what credit is that to you? For even sinners love those who love them (Luke 6:27-32).*

Love your enemies? Do good to those who hate you? Pray for those who mistreat you? None of these are easy, yet we're commanded to do them. It is only with the Love of Christ and obedience to the Holy Spirit that we can carry out such instructions given by Christ.

"This is one important reason *why* Shepherds had to take heed to themselves and to the flock of God. They had to do it because *the Church doesn't belong to them*, it belongs to Jesus who purchased it with His own blood" *(Enduring Word Bible Commentary on Acts 20).*

The Psalmist said, *"Know that the Lord Himself is God; it is He who has made us, and not we ourselves; We are His people and the sheep of His pasture"* *(Psalms. 100:3).*

Consider this, Jesus asked Peter (three times) if he loved Him and commanded him to feed the sheep. In Hebrew culture, saying something three times draws emphasis to what is being said and indicates it is of great significance. Why would Jesus ask three times? Jesus was emphasizing what He was saying to Peter; He wanted Peter to understand the significance of bringing sheep (people) into the sheepfold (Kingdom). Jesus was getting ready to leave His disciples; He was in-between resurrection and ascension.

> *[15] So when they had finished breakfast, Jesus said to Simon Peter, "Simon, son of John, do you love Me more than these?" He said to Him, "Yes, Lord; You know that I love You." He said to him, "Tend My lambs." [16] He said to him again a second time, "Simon, son of John, do you love Me?" He said to Him, "Yes, Lord; You know that I love You." He said to him, "Shepherd My sheep." [17] He said to him the third time, "Simon, son of John, do you love Me?" Peter was grieved because He said to him the third time, "Do you love Me?" And he said to Him, "Lord, You know all things; You know that I love You." Jesus said to him, "Tend My sheep" (John 21:15-19).*

Some versions say, "tend my lambs," "feed my sheep," "shepherd my sheep." Jesus made a distinction between the lamb and the sheep. He emphasized that they all belong to Him. Jesus shed His blood for all. Lambs are as babes; they are tender and vulnerable. Sheep are more mature. This in itself indicates that lambs and sheep are to be 'cared for' in a different manner or at a different level, as an infant to a toddler, a toddler to a preschool-aged child, a child to an adolescent, and ultimately an adolescent to an adult. Therefore, a wise Shepherd will have discernment in caring for the lamb and the sheep accordingly. All sheep do not require the same level of mentoring nor do all adhere to the same level of learning. For this reason, many Churches will choose to divide classes and teach members according to social age or spiritual maturity. Lambs and sheep should be taught at a level commensurate with their understanding. Yet, the goal is for ALL to continue to grow spiritually, ultimately drawing nearer to God. The Apostle Paul said to desire the "sincere milk of the Word," but he also said to move on to the meat and solid food of the spiritually mature:

> *For though by this time you ought to be teachers, you need someone to teach you again the basic principles of the oracles of God. You need milk, not solid food, 13 for everyone who lives on milk is unskilled in the word of righteousness, since he is a child. 14 But solid food is for the mature, for those who have their powers of discernment trained by constant practice to distinguish good from evil (Heb. 5:12-14).*

Outside the Church, if an adult feel insulted by being addressed as a child (or adolescent), he/she will feel insulted in the Church as well. This applies to any age group. Jesus said treat others the way you want to be treated (the Golden Rule, Matt. 7:12). This rule recognizes the respect and dignity of others, whether inside or outside the Body of Christ.

In the Old Testament, God oftentimes used illustrations to send a message out to His people, Israel. These messages are advantageous to us today.

- He used Ezekiel to demonstrate His plan to punish Israel (390 days) and Judah (40 days) because of their guilt.

> *Then lie down on your left side, and I will place on you the guilt of the nation of Israel. For 390 days you will stay there and suffer because of their guilt. I have sentenced you to one day for each year their punishment will last. When you finish that, turn over on your right side and suffer for the guilt of Judah for forty days---one day for each year of their punishment* (Ezek. 4:4-6).

- He used the Prophet Hosea's marriage to Gomer (a prostitute/promiscuous woman) to demonstrate His love and faithfulness to Israel. God compares Himself to a husband with an unfaithful wife, Israel. Yet even when Israel turned from idolatry and repented to God, He forgave them and restored them (Hos. 1-4).

- He used Zechariah to demonstrate a Shepherd (Himself) over a flock (Israel) that was "doomed for slaughter" (about to be judged). Zechariah acted out the prophesy, as Ezekiel and Hosea did in the previous examples. His task was not an easy one. He said "my soul hated them and they hated me." So, he decided to "Let them die! Let them perish!" He broke the two staffs he was using to shepherd them (Favor and Union),

> meaning God was breaking covenant with Israel and He was dividing Israel and Judah (Zech. 11).

Focusing on the third example, this flock which Zechariah pastored was a difficult one. They didn't appreciate him as Shepherd. In fact, according to him "they hated me." They offered him the price of a slave for his services (thirty pieces of silver). God told him not to accept it, but "throw it to the potter." In other words, donate it to the potter's field where the poor are buried. Since they didn't appreciate him as Shepherd, God then instructed Zechariah to act like a foolish shepherd. God would show them what foolish shepherds are like:

> *15 Then the LORD said to me, "Take again the equipment of a foolish shepherd. 16 For I am going to raise up a shepherd over the land who will not care for the lost, or seek the young, or heal the injured, or feed the healthy, but will eat the meat of the choice sheep, tearing off their hooves (Zech. 11:15-16 NIV).*

This Scripture fully describes characteristics of a foolish shepherd, he:

- Will not care for the lost

- Will not seek the young

- Will not heal those who are injured (broken)

- Will not feed the healthy (those who still stand)

- Will eat the meat of the choice sheep, tearing off their hooves"

WOW! A foolish shepherd doesn't care for anyone: the sick, the broken, the young, the old, the dejected, not even the healthy! But God has a day of reckoning for the foolish and worthless shepherds (Zech. 11:17). Jesus reminds us that He is the good Shepherd. He referred to shepherds who did not care for the sheep as "a hired hand."

> [11]*I am the good shepherd; the good shepherd lays down His life for the sheep.* [12] *He who is a hired hand, and not a shepherd, who is not the owner of the sheep, sees the wolf coming, and leaves the sheep and flees, and the wolf snatches them and scatters them.* [13] *He flees because he is a hired hand and is not concerned about the sheep (John 10:11-13).*

God promises in the Restoration of Israel that as a Good Shepherd, He Himself will seek for His sheep, care for them, deliver them, bring them out, and four times He will **feed them:**

The Restoration of Israel

> [11] *For thus says the Lord GOD, "Behold, I Myself will search for My sheep and seek them* [12] *As a shepherd cares for his herd in the day when he is among his scattered sheep, so I will care for My sheep and will deliver them from all the places to which they were scattered on a cloudy and gloomy day.* [13] *I will bring them out from the peoples and gather them from the countries and bring them to their own land; and I will feed them on the mountains of Israel, by the streams, and in all the inhabited places of the land.* [14] *I will feed them in a good pasture, and their grazing ground will be on the mountain heights of Israel. There they will lie down on good grazing ground and feed in rich pasture*

> *on the mountains of Israel. [15] I will feed My flock and I will lead them to rest," declares the Lord GOD. [16] "I will seek the lost, bring back the scattered, bind up the broken and strengthen the sick; but the fat and the strong I will destroy. I will feed them with judgment (Ezek. 34:11-16).*

Pastoral ministry should primarily be one of feeding people the Word of God. The sheep need to remember that God has appointed Shepherds to feed and lead them. The Shepherds need to remember that the flock belongs to God and not to them. Therefore, let us pray for our Shepherds. Their jobs are not easy. Pray that the love of God be imbedded in their hearts for the flock they shepherd. Pray that they would love and pray for the entire flock and not just the preferred flock. Pray that they would be found worthy of the vocation God has called them to walk in, and that they will not be numbered with the "foolish shepherds." Pray God's blessing of patience and endurance upon them. Pray that they would have ears to hear, eyes to see, and discernment to lead the people of God.

Finally, let us pray that they would be counted as good Shepherds described in Ezekiel 34 – one who would seek for His sheep, care for them, deliver them, and bring them out. Pray that they would FEED THE FLOCK, so that the sheep of God's pastures are not "marked for slaughter." It is in the name of Jesus Christ, Name above all names, that we pray. AMEN & AMEN.

CHAPTER 7

Know Those Who Labor Among You

And we beseech you, brethren, to know them which labor among you, and are over you in the Lord, and admonish you; And to esteem them very highly in love for their work's sake. And be at peace among yourselves (I Thes. 5:12-13 KJV).

Now also we beseech you, brethren, get to know those who labor [recognize them for what they are, acknowledge and appreciate and respect them]—your leaders who are over you in the Lord and those who warn and kindly reprove and exhort you. And hold them in very high and most affectionate esteem in [intelligent and sympathetic] appreciation of their work. Be at peace among yourselves (I Thes. 5:12-13 AMP).

As I studied this Scripture, I had a similar feeling that I suspect Luke, a Gentile physician, must have had when he wrote Luke 1:1-4. Luke began by informing his Gentile audience that many had attempted to write about the things which had taken place, but it seemed proper to him to write as well, since he had investigated everything and wanted to give an orderly account:

> *1-4 So many others have tried their hand at putting together a story of the wonderful harvest of Scripture and history that took place among us, using reports handed down by the original eyewitnesses who*

served this Word with their very lives. Since I have investigated all the reports in close detail, starting from the story's beginning, I decided to write it all out for you, most honorable Theophilus, so you can know beyond the shadow of a doubt the reliability of what you were taught (Luke 1:1-4 MSG).

Research has shown that 'many' have written about "Know Those who Labor Among You;" however, it seemed 'fitting' to me to write as well, from both, a Church Leader and a member's perspective.

I have found "under the sun" that despite doing a great work in the name of the Lord, opposition will still come! James says we quarrel and fight (opposition) because of 'desires that battle within us' (James 4:1). I submit to you that jealousy, envy, strife, insecurity and unresolved conflict among other things, causes "battles within us." If there is a battle going on within, how can there not be a battle going on without? How can we love others when we struggle with loving ourselves? How can we love God whom we have not seen and hate our brother whom we have seen? (1 John 4:20). Jesus did great works, still opposition came. Paul, Silas and Timothy had no evil intentions or secret plans for their own benefit. They only desired to do what the Lord called them to do, yet they faced opposition from Church Leaders.

Opposition in Ministry

The Apostle Paul founded the Church at Thessalonica and ministered there along with Silas and Timothy. These three were doing a great work in Thessalonica. Souls were being saved, Jews and Greeks alike. People were converting from paganism. God-fearing Greeks and a number of 'leading women' were persuaded by Paul and Silas. They joyfully received the Gospel that comes from the Holy Spirit even in the midst of persecution (Acts 17:1-4; 1 Thes. 2). The Church at Thessalonica became a model Church as they had turned from idols to serve the living God. Paul insisted it was the work of the Holy Spirit (1 Thes. 1:5-9).

In spite of the great works, Paul faced great opposition from the Jews and was driven out. Paul said they hindered him from speaking to the Gentiles (1 Thes. 2:15-16). Scripture says the Jews became jealous, formed a mob and set the city in an uproar (Acts 17:5). The opposition from the Jewish leaders was so great that Paul fled and ministered in other places in Greece: Berea, Athens, Corinth (Acts 17-18), and was joined later by Silas and Timothy (Acts 18:5). When Paul sent Timothy to check on the Church at Thessalonica (1 Thes. 3:1-5), Timothy returned with a report that the Church was being persecuted and Jewish people were saying bad things about Paul, that his intentions were wrong and that he was preaching for profit or personal gain. They were saying that Paul and his friends (Silas and Timothy) had behaved badly and that he didn't care about the people. Paul (along with Silas and Timothy) wrote the letter to the Church at Thessalonica to encourage them and to answer the false accusations (1 Thes. 2:5-8).

In spite of Paul, Timothy and Silas doing the work they were called and anointed to do, opposition still arose from Jewish leaders out of jealousy. Jealousy has existed from the fall of Satan out of Heaven and still exists in our Churches today. Oh, what a powerful force the Church would be if leaders would rally around one another and support the work of the Ministry in winning souls to Christ! This is what Jesus commissioned His disciples to do:

> *Go into all the world and make disciples of all nations,*
> *baptizing them in the name of the Father and of the Son*
> *and of the Holy Spirit, teaching them to observe all that*
> *I commanded you (Matt. 28:19).*

When jealousy and envy are present when a team goes out to do His work, they are treated as castaways or enemies and perceived by Church Leaders to be disloyal. Yet, the Church continues to pray for unity in the Body of Christ! Know those who labor among you. Jesus said, "I have other sheep, which are not of this fold" (John 10:16). The Wycliff Bible Commentary holds that Jesus was referring to the Gentiles who would respond to the Gospel and they would become one-fold with the Jews (Pfeiffer & Harrison p.1095). However, I'd like to expand that thought and say, ALL of His sheep are not in one place (one Church); Jesus laid down His life for ALL sheep. God's mission is the same in all Christian Churches, to make disciples of Him. When the Body of Christ realizes that we're not enemies but on the same team, it will function more harmoniously, all parts working together as one. If we all had the attitude of the Apostle Paul, "as long as Christ is preached, I will rejoice," the Body of Christ would be much more effective in winning souls. This in itself, is unity. Consider:

- Jehoshaphat trusted his men to teach (2 Chron. 17:7-9).

- Jesus sent His twelve disciples out two-by-two to minister (Mark 6:7).

- Jesus commissioned his disciples to go and make disciples of all nations (Matt. 28:19).

- Jesus appointed seventy others to go before Him in pairs "for the harvest is plentiful, but the laborers are few" (Luke 10:1-2).

- The church sent out Preachers to preach the Word (Roman. 10:13-15).

- Paul sent Timothy out to check on the Church at Thessalonica (1 Thes. 3:1-5).

ALL of the work of the ministry is not within the four walls of the Church! Leaders must know and trust the ones they've mentored and trained to go outside the walls of the Church; likewise, members must be able to trust their leaders.

Interestingly, the words "to know" in 1 Thes 5:12 translates differently across Bible versions: the NIV says "to acknowledge," the NASB says "to appreciate," and the NLT says, "to honor." I believe the Apostle Paul was instructing the church members to do all of the above regarding their leaders for the work they do. Leadership pertains to all who share in leadership responsibilities. This includes but is not limited to Bishops, Pastors, Associate Pastors, Elders, Deacons, Ministers, and Lay-Leaders according to the establishment of the Church. Some leaders are paid employees of the Church, while others work tirelessly "as unto the Lord" without pay. How much more are they to be esteemed and appreciated!

So then, if church members are to love, honor, respect, know, appreciate, recognize, and esteem their Leaders, does this exempt Leaders from reciprocating the same to its members? I say "Nay verily" (KJV). Leadership has equal responsibility to its members. This includes but is not limited to:

- Teach sound doctrine, those of our Lord and Savior Jesus Christ (1 Tim. 6:3).

- Be an example in character (1 Tim. 3: 4-11).

- Be unbiased, doing nothing in the spirit of partiality; not show favoritism (Gal. 2:6; James 2).

- Pray for the flock and keep watch over their souls (Heb. 13:17).

- Warn those who are unruly, comfort the fainthearted, uphold the weak, be patient with all (1 Thes. 5:13-14).

Matthew Henry Commentary provides the following summary of Leadership and Membership responsibilities, in which he refers to leaders as Ministers:

Leadership Responsibilities

1. Ministers must labor among their people, labor with diligence, and unto weariness; they must labor in the Word and doctrine (1 Tim. 5:17).

2. They are called laborers and should not be loiterers. They must labor with their people, to instruct, comfort, and edify them.

3. Ministers are to rule their people also, so the word is rendered (1 Tim. 5:17). They must rule, not with rigor, but with love. They must not exercise dominion as temporal lords; but rule as spiritual guides, by setting a good example to the flock. They are over the people in the Lord, to distinguish them from civil magistrates, and to denote also that they are but ministers

under Christ, appointed by him, and must rule the people by Christ's laws, and not by laws of their own. This may also intimate the end of their office and all their labor; namely, the service and honor of the Lord.

4. They must also admonish the people, and that not only publicly, but privately, as there may be occasion. They must instruct them to do well and should reprove when they do ill. It is their duty not only to give good counsel, but also to give admonition, to give warning to the flock of the dangers they are liable to and reprove for negligence or what else may be amiss.

Membership Responsibilities

1. The people must know them. As the shepherd should know his flock, so the sheep must know their shepherd. They must know his person, hear his voice, acknowledge him for their pastor, and pay due regard to his teaching, ruling, and admonitions.

2. They must esteem their ministers highly in love. They should greatly value the office of the ministry, honor and love the persons of their ministers. They should show them esteem and affection in all proper ways for their work's sake, because their business is to promote the honor of Christ and the welfare of men's souls.

He concludes with "there is a mutual duty between minister and the people - To promote the honor of Christ and the welfare of men's souls" (Matthew Henry Commentary on 1 Thes. 5).

Likewise, the Apostle Paul admonished the Church at Thessalonica to give respect and honor to those who lead and work for their benefit, their Leaders. For it is the Leaders' task to care for the Church, to correct and guide it in the right way, and to promote unity among members. Therefore, he wanted the members to love and support them (1 Thes. 5:12-13).

Inappropriate or Misfit Leadership

I have found "under the sun" during my years of ministry, one sure thing that causes division, strife, or discard in the Body of Christ. It affects the flow of service, even the anointing. This is the practice of appointing members to positions where they are not apt or called! This may happen for various reasons. Perhaps there are not enough members in the Church to occupy positions needed, so members are appointed out of necessity. Oftentimes members are appointed due to relationship of the appointed to the appointee. Another classic example is that of members appointed as an act of favoritism. Still, members may be appointed due to their "financial status," and their ability to give BIG to the Church. Whatever the reason, Scripture cites examples of disaster happening when the wrong people are appointed to positions:

- God instructed Moses to appoint the sons of Kohath (Levites) to carry the Ark of the Covenant (Num. 4:15; Deut. 10:8). He told them to carry the Ark on their shoulders, using poles that would be placed through rings attached to the four corners of the Ark (Ex 25:13-14; Nu 7:9). However, when David attempted to bring the Ark from Kiriath-jearim (Judah) to Jerusalem, the Ark was placed on a cart and driven by Uzzah and Ahio, the sons of Abinadab, who were not of the sons of Kohath (II Sam. 6:3; 2 Chron 29:12). At one point, the oxen shook the cart and Uzzah touched the Ark (which was forbidden) and he died for his irreverence (2 Sam 6:6-7).

- Aaron and his sons, descendants of Levi, were ordained to serve as Priests (Num. 3:3). However, Jeroboam (King of Israel) appointed priests "from all sorts of people," not from the descendants of Aaron the high priest and led Israel into idolatry (1 Ki. 13:33-34). This was the sin of Jeroboam which led to his downfall; he and his entire household perished (1 Ki. 15:29-30).

- Uzziah, King of Judah, reigned fifty-two years in Jerusalem. Scripture says "when he became strong, his heart was so proud that he acted corruptly and he was unfaithful to the Lord his God, for he entered the temple of the Lord to burn incense on the altar of incense (2 Chron. 26:16). The Priests tried to deter him, but he would not listen, he became enraged with the Priests. Because of this act, he was struck with leprosy to the day of his death (2 Chron. 26:21). The King exemplified "misfit leadership," as he was not authorized to burn incense in the temple. Only Aaron and his sons (Levites) were appointed by law to burn incense (Ex 30:7).

Obviously, it is important to God that careful attention be given when appointing people to different positions. God is a God of order and He operates in perfection. Why would He desire any less? God is a Holy God and requires us to be holy.

King David understood order and reverence for the things of God. He appointed musicians and singers to minister in the house of the Lord. He 'set apart' the sons of Asaph, Heman and Jeduthun who were trained and skillful (1 Chron 25:1, 7). They ministered with song before the tabernacle of the tent of meeting, until Solomon had built the house of the LORD in Jerusalem; and they served in their office according to their order (1 Chron. 6:32).

Upon the death of King David, Solomon built the Temple and followed in his Father's footsteps, appointing the same order of musicians:

> *12 and all the Levitical singers, Asaph, Heman, Jeduthun, and their sons and kinsmen, clothed in fine linen, with cymbals, harps and lyres, standing east of the altar, and with them one hundred and twenty priests blowing trumpets 13 in unison when the trumpeters and the singers were to make themselves heard with one voice to praise and to glorify the LORD, and when they lifted up their voice accompanied by trumpets and cymbals and instruments of music, and when they praised the LORD saying, "He indeed is good for His lovingkindness is everlasting," then the house, the house of the LORD, was filled with a cloud, 14 so that the priests could not stand to minister because of the cloud, for the glory of the LORD filled the house of God (2 Chron. 5:12-14).*

So, the singers and musicians were appointed, set apart, trained, and skilled. They served according to their order, in unison with one voice, to praise and glorify the Lord according to the laws set before them. As a result, the glory of God filled the Temple, the house of God, so much that the Priests could not stand to minister. When Church Leaders return to enforcing a standard of Holiness on its musicians and singers, those appointed to usher in the presence of the Lord, as the Levitical singers and musicians did, the glory of God will return!

In an article by John D. Risser, Know Them Which Labor Among You (2017), Mr. Risser addresses such concerns as: what should church leaders do to gain the respect of their people? What should the people do when Godly church leaders appear to be going wrong? What forms of church leadership and practical administrations follow biblical directives? J. D. Risser offers the following in regard to those placed in spiritual authority as church leaders:

1. Recognize that all authority is God-ordained (Rom. 13:1-2).

2. Past relationships are important as well as their ability to develop and maintain healthy ongoing relationships with integrity.

3. When earthly leaders require that the people under their authority make decisions or act in ways which are contrary to the higher written law of God, disobedience to their laws is necessary in order to continue living as true followers of God and His Word. However, there must still always be honor and respect through it all.

4. There are those instances when a believer realizes that he is no longer able, with a clear conscience, to be in harmony with the specific ways his local church applies the teachings of Scripture. At this juncture in his life, he should seek out a church with which he can once more voluntarily cast his lot.

5. It is a weakness of humanity to view any authority either with too much reverence or with disdain. As believers, we seek to find God's will in this delicate balancing act. Those who "labor among us" have not campaigned nor fought for their position, as many in earthly kingdoms do. Rather, they have been given a duty of service (by God) that has changed their life forever.

6. As Leaders seek to fulfill the duties God has given them through the church, their desire should be to "know them [those]" under their authority. This is necessary to help them determine the spiritual condition of those believers, so they can "watch for their souls."

7. In relating to spiritual authorities, it is just as improper for us to revere them as it is to disrespect them. To understand, bless, and encourage them, we need to realize that they are still living in the flesh, with similar struggles as those faced by the rest of us. With all this in mind, we see then that their responsibility also brings added accountability.

8. Open communication with them about our lives is imperative in helping them to continue their work. Asking them about their spiritual journey is also important. This will give us direct knowledge about how to more properly pray for them from day to day.

9. Those who "labor among us" need friends. It has sometimes happened in Church culture that the ordained men were thought of as ones with whom we can no longer be friends, but rather have more of a "business-style" relationship. This is far from the direction that Scripture gives to believers working together for the glory of God.

10. There are different issues that will always put stress on the godly relationships we should be having with our leaders: disagreements without love, strife among fellow believers, and struggles in interpersonal relationships. Any of these types of struggles always has the potential to bring division to the body.

J. D. Risser concludes with, "A godly Church Leader will spend much time and energy to know the truth about matters and seek to bring any necessary restoration. This will create many temptations for bitterness and cynicism in a leader's experience. He may struggle to love his brethren as he ought, yet he knows that the standard of God has never changed, and he must be faithful in his calling. On our part, as those who are under their authority, we need to give diligence in our personal commitment on holy living and loving the brethren. This then, will be a tremendous asset in bringing about closeness of relationship with *"those who labor among us" (Risser 2-4)*.

CHAPTER 8

Suffer the Little Children

Jesus Blesses Little Children

[13] Then were there brought unto him little children, that he should put his hands on them, and pray: and the disciples rebuked them. [14] But Jesus said, Suffer little children, and forbid them not, to come unto me: for of such is the kingdom of heaven. [15] And he laid his hands on them, and departed thence (Matt. 19:13-15 KJV).

[13] Then some children were brought to Him so that He might lay His hands on them and pray; and the disciples rebuked them. [14] But Jesus said, "Let the children alone, and do not hinder them from coming to Me; for the kingdom of heaven belongs to such as these." [15] After laying His hands on them, He departed from there (Matt. 19:13-15)

Jesus loves children and always acknowledged them. He wanted to be around them, and He took time to pray for them. The disciples wanted to exclude them, but Jesus said, "let them come." This speaks of His character. In fact, he told the adults to be like children. He said unless we change (be converted) and come to Him as a little child, we will never enter the Kingdom of Heaven:

> *At that time the disciples came to Jesus and said, "Who then is greatest in the kingdom of heaven?" ² And He called a child to Himself and set him before them, ³ and said, "Truly I say to you, unless you are converted and become like children, you will not enter the kingdom of heaven. ⁴ Whoever then humbles himself as this child, he is the greatest in the kingdom of heaven. ⁵ And whoever receives one such child in My name receives Me; ⁶ but whoever causes one of these little ones who believe in Me to stumble, it would be better for him to have a heavy millstone hung around his neck, and to be drowned in the depth of the sea (Matt. 18:1-6).*

This was His response to His disciples asking Him who is greatest in the Kingdom of Heaven. In essence, Jesus was saying whoever takes the lowly position of this child is the greatest in the Kingdom of Heaven. Jesus is teaching on humility and acceptance. He was teaching His disciples to be humble, not to desire to be the greatest but to walk in humility as a little child. *Humility is the fear of the Lord; its wages are riches, honor, and life (Pr. 22:4).* He was further teaching them not to 'exclude' what He has included or accepted.

> *³⁶ Taking a child, He set him before them, and taking him in His arms, He said to them, ³⁷ "Whoever receives one child like this in My name receives Me; and*

whoever receives Me does not receive Me, but Him who sent Me" (Mark 9:36-37).

Do we make the same mistakes in the Church today as the disciples did? Do we seek greatness in the Kingdom of *the Church*? Do we exclude children from participating in Church ministries? Do we pick and choose 'which children' will participate and select the same children over and over again? This may very well send a message to a child that indeed you *are* the greatest among the children. Likewise, it may send a negative message to the one least likely to be selected that "you are not good enough." Such a message can crush a little one's spirit. Jesus said it would be better to have a heavy millstone hung around your neck and to be drowned in the depth of the sea than to cause little ones who believe in Him to stumble. Stumbling does not imply tripping over a rock. It does imply that emotional damages can result when a spirit is crushed. He also said not to despise the little ones, *"for their angels in heaven continually see the face of His Father in heaven" (Matt. 18:10).*

The same spiritual brokenness can also apply to adults, babes in Christ, strangers, and people who are less fortunate. Society's outcasts can be viewed as "little" in the eyes of some. However, Jesus said whatever you did/did not do for the least of these, you did/did not do for Me (Matt. 25:40, 45). Whether the ill treatment is due to cultural background, race, creed, gender, parent's socio-economic status or other reason, know that God hates partiality and He is not in the spirit-crushing business.

> [22] *A joyful heart is good medicine, but a broken spirit dries up the bones (Pr. 17:22).*

To the pre-millennials, can you recall games played in school whereby Team Captains were selected (oftentimes teacher's pets as referred) and the Captains would select team members for the purpose of competitions? Students would sit and wait to be selected. If you were ever the last or among the last to be selected, can you recall that feeling?

Here's another one. Can you recall school plays whereby the leading characters were always assigned to the "preferred or favored students" and IF you were given a part in the play it was an 'insignificant' part? If you were NOT selected to be in the play, remember the feeling of not making the cut?

Lastly, in high school, do you remember not making the basketball, football or other team, not because you lacked skill, but because the "preferred or favored" students were selected? Sometimes selections were based on their parent's relationship with the coaches, or a parent's level of participation with activities such as the Parent/Teachers Association (PTA) which brought funds to the school. Remember the feeling?

Such feelings apply to adults as well. Do you remember being "passed over" for a job you were most qualified for? Do you remember having to train the person selected for the job by nature of relationship with the hiring official? Do you remember the lack of justice displayed on your behalf? Do you remember your feelings related to the new hire and the hiring official?

Rejection happens at all levels; however, this chapter's focus is on "little children," particularly the less fortunate and those without a voice. Rejection hurts! Whether it is done intentionally or unintentionally, it leaves undesired memories. It leaves the feeling of

"I'm not good enough" and promotes low self-esteem. Rejection happens in and outside the Church. However, as Christians we are called to a higher standard. Impartiality, unfair treatment of children and showing favoritism is unbecoming of Christian behavior.

> *The spirit of a man will sustain his infirmity; but a wounded spirit who can bear? (Pr. 18:14).*

In other words, emotional and spiritual suffering is much harder to endure than physical suffering. We should be more careful not to wound a child's spirit, or the spirit of man. Physical wounds heal and often do not leave scars. Emotional or spiritual wounds tend to leave its mark and is often irreversible, without God's assistance. God can break the spirit of man, but His breaking draws us closer to Him.

> *The sacrifices of God are a broken spirit; A broken and a contrite heart, O God, You will not despise (Ps. 51:17).*

To the Parents of any children who have been rejected, overlooked, slighted, left out, considered "least among other children," whether in Church or outside Church, pray for and forgive those whose actions may have caused it. This may apply to you, the parent: negative parental practices are often repeated to the next generation. Remember the Word of the Lord and pronounce them over your children:

> *The Lord is near to the broken hearted, and saves those who are crushed in spirit (Ps. 34:18).*

> *He heals the broken hearted and binds up their wounds (Ps. 147:3).*

Behold, children are a gift of the LORD,
The fruit of the womb is a reward.
⁴ Like arrows in the hand of a warrior,
So are the children of one's youth.

⁵ How blessed is the man whose quiver is full of them;
They will not be ashamed when they speak with their
enemies in the gate (Ps. 127:3-5).

From the mouth of infants and nursing babes You
have established strength because of Your
adversaries, to make the enemy and the revengeful
cease (Ps. 8:2).

⁴ Fathers, do not provoke your children to anger, but
bring them up in the discipline and instruction of the
Lord (Eph. 6:4).

Just as Jesus welcomed children, made them feel important, and protected them, so should we! All children are our responsibility. This is an imperfect world and each of us can remember a lingering insult, hurt, and rejection. For a child who is carrying this burden, let us be the one who intervenes and helps to break that cycle of rejection. Leave a legacy in the hearts of the little ones, every one of them.

CHAPTER 9

How Do You Define "L-O-Y-A-L-T-Y?"

Merriam-Webster dictionary defines loyalty as "unswerving in allegiance," such as:

a) faithful in allegiance to one's lawful sovereign or government (loyal to a king);

b) faithful to a private person to whom faithfulness is due (a loyal husband);

c) faithful to a cause, ideal, custom, institution, or product (a loyal churchgoer; loyal to the party of their forebears).

T his chapter will cover two types of Loyalty: "**unfeigned**" and "**feigned**" loyalty. **Unfeigned** loyalty is one that is genuine, sincere, and without hypocrisy. On the contrary, **feigned** loyalty represents loyalty which is not genuine, not real, dishonest, pretended or simulated; To represent fictitiously; to put on an appearance of loyalty while their actions are deceptive to others (Merriam-Webster Dictionary, 1983). By the end of this chapter you will be able to identify true loyalty and not be misguided by hypocrisy.

Examples of Unfeigned Loyalty

Ruth's loyalty to Naomi in the book of Ruth is a classic and beautiful example of unfeigned loyalty. As the story goes, Naomi had sojourned with her husband (Elimelech) and her two sons (Mahlon and Chilion) from Bethlehem in Judah to the land of Moab due to famine in the land. While there, her sons intermarry Moabite women (Orpah and Ruth). Naomi's husband and her two sons die in Moab, so she returns to Bethlehem, as the famine is now over. She encourages her daughters-in-law to remain in the land of Moab. Orpah returned to Moab, however Ruth refused to leave Naomi. Ruth's loyalty to Naomi is reflected in *Ruth 1:16-17:*

> *16 But Ruth said, "Do not urge me to leave you or turn back from following you; for where you go, I will go, and where you lodge, I will lodge. Your people shall be my people, and your God, my God. 17 Where you die, I will die, and there I will be buried. Thus, may the LORD do to me, and worse, if anything but death parts you and me." 18 When she saw that she was determined to go with her, she said no more to her.*

So, Ruth returns to Judah with Naomi and is blessed for her loyalty. As the story ends, she marries a relative of Naomi (Boaz), has a son (Obed), who fathers a son (Jesse), who fathers a son (King David), an ancestor of our Messiah, Jesus Christ. God blesses true loyalty.

A **second example** of unfeigned loyalty is that of Jonathan's loyalty to David (1 Sam. 20). Jonathan's father, King Saul, was jealous of David (who was anointed by Samuel to succeed him as King of Israel). The King sought to kill David. However, Jonathan's loyalty and friendship with David caused him to protect David and to inform him of his father's plans. Jonathan made a covenant with the house of

David and vowed that the Lord be between them and their descendants forever.

> *Jonathan said to David, "Go in safety, inasmuch as we have sworn to each other in the name of the LORD, saying, 'The LORD will be between me and you, and between my descendants and your descendants forever'." Then he rose and departed, while Jonathan went into the city (1 Sam. 20:42).*

Jonathan recognized that his father (King Saul) had no cause to hate David or take his life. He questioned his own Father's evil motives (1 Sam. 20:32) and remained loyal to his friend David. As the story ends, Jonathan and his father were killed in battle. David became King of Israel and honored his vow to Jonathan by showing kindness to his son, Mephibosheth:

> *[6] Mephibosheth, the son of Jonathan the son of Saul, came to David and fell on his face and prostrated himself. And David said, "Mephibosheth." And he said, "Here is your servant!" [7] David said to him, "Do not fear, for I will surely show kindness to you for the sake of your father Jonathan, and will restore to you all the land of your grandfather Saul; and you shall eat at my table regularly." [8] Again he prostrated himself and said, "What is your servant, that you should regard a dead dog like me?" [9] Then the king called Saul's servant Ziba and said to him, "All that belonged to Saul and to all his house I have given to your master's grandson. [10] You and your sons and your servants shall cultivate the land for him, and you shall bring in the produce so that your master's grandson*

> *may have food; nevertheless, Mephibosheth your*
> *master's grandson shall eat at my table regularly (2*
> *Sam. 9:6-10).*

Examples of Feigned Loyalty

An example of feigned loyalty is seen in 1 Sam. 21-22, the story of King Saul and his Chief of Herdsmen, Doeg the Edomite. King Saul had obviously convinced himself that David was his enemy and was out to kill him. David runs from King Saul and stops at the house of Ahimelech, the High Priest who lived in Nob. Ahimelech assisted David by giving him consecrated bread and the sword of Goliath. Doeg witnessed the interaction and later informed King Saul (1 Sam. 22:9). When King Saul questioned Ahimelech and accused David of wrongdoings, Ahimelech elected not to assassinate the character of David, but instead showed unfeigned loyalty to him. The High Priest reminded King Saul of David's faithfulness and trustworthiness to him (1 Sam 22:14). King Saul, in his anger, is determined to believe otherwise. He ordered the murder of Ahimelech and all the Priests of Nob, but his servants refuse to carry out this order. Doeg the Edomite carried out the order and slayed Ahimelech and all the Priests of Nob (85 in all), their families and livestock in Nob, the city of the Priests (1 Sam. 22: 18-19).

Consider, **WHY** was Doeg the Edomite adamant about carrying out the King's order?   On the surface, one can surmise that Doeg was being loyal to King Saul by carrying out his order. When King Saul's servants declined the order, Doeg executed it! We get a better understanding of this relationship by reading Psalms 52 (NIV), where David describes the "feigned loyalty" exemplified by Doeg the Edomite:

Psalm 52

For the director of music. A *maskil of* David. When Doeg the Edomite had gone to Saul and told him: "David has gone to the house of Ahimelech."

[1] Why do you boast of evil, you mighty hero?
Why do you boast all day long,
you who are a disgrace in the eyes of God?

[2] You who practice deceit,
your tongue plots destruction;
it is like a sharpened razor.

[3] You love evil rather than good,
falsehood rather than speaking the truth

[4] You love every harmful word,
you deceitful tongue!

[5] Surely God will bring you down to everlasting ruin:
He will snatch you up and pluck you from your tent;
he will uproot you from the land of the living.

[6] The righteous will see and fear;
they will laugh at you, saying,

[7] "Here now is the man
who did not make God his stronghold
but trusted in his great wealth
and grew strong by destroying others!"

David describes Doeg as one who boasts of evil, practices deceit, and loves evil rather than good. Further, Doeg had a deceitful tongue, did not make God his stronghold, trusted in his great wealth, and grew strong by destroying others! Well, anyone can see David and Doeg are not friends! Unlike the Priest Ahimelech, Doeg certainly had no allegiance to David. According to Rabbinical Literature, "Doeg's most unfortunate qualities were malice, jealousy, and a *calumnious* (slanderous) tongue. He carried a grudge against David, whose opinion prevailed over his own in determining the site for the Temple at Jerusalem. Doeg is depicted as an antagonist of David. (*Jewish Encyclopedia. com>5254>(Zeb 54b). Doeg).* There was no exhibition of loyalty here!

Hence the question, ***"How do you define Loyalty?"*** What does loyalty look like to you? *Feigned* loyalty is seen in corporate America, government, civilian jobs, schools, and sadly, in our Churches, where 'some grow strong by destroying others' (Ps. 52:7). I submit that Doeg, the Edomite, had his own interest in mind, and getting rid of David would have possibly positioned him in a closer relationship to the King. He was a chief herdsman. David was a mighty warrior who ate at the King's table and was best friends with the King's son, Jonathan.

Have you passed up an opportunity to defend a brother or sister in Christ for selfish gain? Have you scandalized others in the Body of Christ, or allowed them to be scandalized, for the sake of position? Have you listened and did not defend those in leadership while others scandalized their person? Have you ever engaged in an unethical behavior for the sake of gaining a position or attempting to move closer to the esteemed leader? This I have witnessed "under the sun."

We constantly hear about the spirit of Jezebel and the spirit of Absalom in our churches. We seldom if ever hear about the spirit of Doeg. It is alive and runs rampant. Allow me to expose it.

Characteristics of the spirit of Doeg

- The spirit of Doeg will expose others (rather than cover them) so it can shine, or, for selfish gain.

  o Doeg exposed David (1 Sam. 22:9-10).

- The spirit of Doeg will do anything it is told to do, right or wrong, to "appear" to be loyal to a Leader.

  o When the servants refused to kill Ahimelech and the other Priests, Doeg seized the opportunity to gain favor with the King by killing 85 Priests in all (1 Sam. 22:18).

- The spirit of Doeg will slay innocent people for personal gain.

  o Doeg killed the families and livestock of the Priests (men, women, children, babies, oxen, donkeys, and sheep (1 Sam. 22:19).

- The spirit of Doeg is NOT true loyalty. It is an illusion of loyalty, with a motive. This is feigned loyalty.

  o Doeg was jealous of David and was looking out for his own personal interests (JewishEncyclopedia.com_Doeg).

A **second** example of "feigned" loyalty is seen at 1 Kings Chap 1. When David was old and on his death bed, his son, Adonijah, set himself up as King over Israel. Understand that Adonijah was not David's choice to succeed him as King, his other son Solomon was. Yet Joab (David's Commander over his Hebrew Army) and Abiathar (David's Priest) supported Adonijah and attended a celebration in his honor. But Nathan the Prophet, Benaiah (David's personal guard), and Solomon (David's son) were not invited. They were genuinely loyal to David. I submit to you that Joab and Abiathar were only loyal to their *positions.* No special allegiance was given to God or to King David. They would have betrayed anyone to protect and maintain their position!

Sometimes it appears that people get away with unfair treatment of others. However, in the case of David's officials, the opposite proved true. In fact, on his death bed King David reminded Solomon of Joab's betrayal to him and his evil doings, how he killed two good Generals during peace time. Joab and his men also killed David's son (Absalom) when David specifically charged the Army NOT to kill him (2 Samuel 18:14-15). David charged Solomon not to let his grey hair go down to Sheol in peace (1 Ki. 2:5-6).

Regarding Shimei the Benjamite who had cursed David violently when he was fleeing Absalom, David instructed Solomon, *"do not let him go unpunished, for you are a wise man; and you will know what you ought to do to him, and you will bring his gray hair down to Sheol with blood" (1 Ki. 2:8-9).* However, David instructed Solomon to *"show kindness to the sons of Barzillai the Gileadite, and let them be among those who eat at your table; for they assisted me when I fled from Absalom your brother (I Ki. 2:7).* As the story continues, we see that Solomon "got" the ones to be gotten according to his Father's instructions. Adonijah, Joab, and Shimei were executed (1 Ki. 2:19-46). Solomon maintained as his officials the ones who had been loyal to his father (1 Ki. 5). He showed mercy to Abiathar the Priest but still dismissed him from duties.

> [26] *Then to Abiathar the priest the king said, "Go to Anathoth to your own field, for you deserve to die; but I will not put you to death at this time, because you carried the ark of the Lord GOD before my father David, and because you were afflicted in everything with which my father was afflicted. "* [27] *So Solomon dismissed Abiathar from being priest to the* LORD, *in order to fulfill the word of the* LORD, *which He had spoken concerning the house of Eli in Shiloh (1 Ki. 2:26-27).*

I submit to you, my readers and Church members, that "growing strong by destroying others" is not God's way. *For promotion cometh neither from the east, nor from the west, nor from the south. But God is the judge: he putteth down one, and setteth up another (Ps. 75:6-7 KJV).*

Therefore, do not let your loyalty be driven by malice, jealousy, a desire to be accepted or to gain favor or position from any Leader. Remember the golden rule: treat others the way you want to be treated. Wait on the Lord! In due time, He will exalt you. Your gift will make room for you. Be careful how you define **L-O-Y-A-L-T-Y.**

CHAPTER 10

Promoting A Culture of Compliance

During my years as a civil service worker, I had the opportunity to work in the "Compliance" Section of the Organization. We were preparing for an inspection from higher headquarters and the Commander wanted to ensure the Organization was "inspection-ready." I was selected as a member of the Compliance Team. It was our responsibility to inspect every section of the Organization to ensure our operations were "compliant" with established Policies, Guidance, Instructions, and Manuals of higher authorities.

We were not the most welcomed group as we entered the various sections to conduct inspections. It was not uncommon to be greeted with "Oh no! Here they come again!" Instead of viewing the Compliance Team as a necessary and helpful 'part' of the organization, there to assist the other parts, many viewed us as adversaries with the power of the pin, to expose their shortcomings. They didn't care to understand that we were *one* Team. If one part does badly, it affects the whole. Early on, they didn't understand that what one section does impacts another section. Being scrutinized and placed under the microscope was not a good feeling, but the importance of all sections working together as one was a key factor to our success!

Of the Body of Christ, the Apostle Paul says the body is *one* and yet has many members, and all the members of the body, though they are many, are one body (1 Cor. 12:12). He uses the physical body to illustrate the interdependence of its parts:

> *[20] But now there are many members, but one body. [21] And the eye cannot say to the hand, "I have no need of you"; or again the head to the feet, "I have no need of you." [22] On the contrary, it is much truer that the members of the body which seem to be weaker are necessary; [23] and those members of the body which we deem less honorable, on these we bestow more abundant honor, and our less presentable members become much more presentable, [24] whereas our more presentable members have no need of it. But God has so composed the body, giving more abundant honor to that member which lacked, [25] so that there may be no division in the body, but that the members may have the same care for one another (1 Cor. 12:20-25).*

So, the goal of the Compliance Team was to ensure the organization worked together as a whole, not just in the face of an inspection, but in its day-to-day operation. After one year of inspections and write-ups, education and training, reports and corrections, the organizational parts came together as *one*. All sections had recognized their interdependence. With the entire organization working together as one, we received an OUTSTANDING rating on the inspection by Higher Headquarters due to the attitude and *"culture of compliance"* created. The realization that each section was a part of the same organization, following the same mission and vision, was a concept that had to be embraced to become a winning team.

Just as a culture of compliance is vital to the success of a corporate, private, or federal agency, it is as equally as important to the success of a Church. A culture of compliance is necessary in the Church, which is referred to as a Body, with Christ as the Head (Rom. 12:5; 1 Cor. 12:27; Col. 1:24).

David was the King over Israel for 40 years. God promised him that his descendants would forever sit on the throne as King over Israel. Just before his death, David charged his son Solomon, his successor to the throne, with the following:

> *³ Keep the charge of the LORD your God, to walk in His ways, to keep His statutes, His commandments, His ordinances, and His testimonies, according to what is written in the Law of Moses, that you may succeed in all that you do and wherever you turn, ⁴ so that the LORD may carry out His promise which He spoke concerning me, saying, 'If your sons are careful of their way, to walk before Me in truth with all their heart and with all their soul, you shall not lack a man on the throne of Israel' (1 Ki. 2:3-4).*

In his charge to Solomon, David recognized the need for compliance with God's laws, statutes, commandments, and ordinances in order for him to succeed. He also reminded Solomon of God's requirement that he "walk before Him in truth with all his heart and with all his soul." After becoming King, Solomon prayed to God for an understanding heart to judge His people. He also prayed to be able to discern between good and evil (wisdom). In answer to his prayer for wisdom, God reminded Solomon of His compliance requirement to "walk in My ways, keeping My statutes and commandments as your Father David walked." Afterwards, He would prolong Solomon's days (1 Kings 3:14). Both (God and King David) instilled the necessity of 'compliance' in Solomon as a Leader. Compliance sets behavioral expectations for Leaders and members. When Leaders are compliant, it sets the standard for a culture of compliance among members.

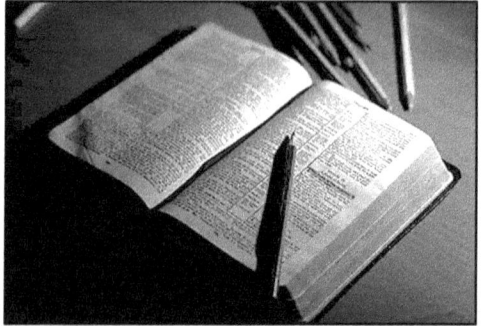

Merriam-Webster's definition of culture is "the set of enduring and underlying assumptions and norms that determine how things are actually done in the organization." Different companies assess the culture of their organization in different ways. While working for the County for seventeen years, I can recall open forums with the Chief Executive Officer (CEO), lunch-and-learn sessions with the Assistant CEO, and private surveys assessing the member's well-being. These were all geared towards assessing the climate and morale of the organization. The forums gave members a 'voice.' We were free to address any organizational issue. It also provided Leaders an opportunity to "know those who labored among them." My experience working for the Federal government provided reviews in a more formal, orderly fashion, also with a forum which encouraged dialogue. Review of performance objectives, measures and metrics was a means for supervisors and employees to dialogue. Employees were made aware of job expectations and had access to communicate with their raters beforehand to avoid upset at rating time.

How do we ensure compliance in the Church? Some Churches may hold meetings involving Leadership only. Some may have participatory-type meetings whereby the entire congregation is afforded the opportunity to discuss the goals and direction of the

Church. Some may have lecture-style meetings which offer no input from the members. It's strictly a "this is the way it's going to go" meeting. Sadly, some Churches may never have meetings with its members. In spite of various methods applied, a culture of compliance CANNOT exist without open, honest communication.

Philip Naughton (Head of UK Compliance at Cordium) describes in an article, *Compliance Culture: Building an Approach on Three Core Values (31 August 2018),* 3 core values essential to a culture of compliance: **Fairness, Transparency, and Diversity**. The article targets Corporate and Investment companies; however, for the sake of this chapter I will use this model and relate it to Compliance within a Church setting. The following are excerpts from the article, and for the sake of brevity, presented in abbreviated form:

1. **Fairness** - ensuring fair outcomes across the range of stakeholders an organization may have. The rules serve as recognition that the decisions a single employee makes can have profound consequences for the community as a whole. Examples:

   - **Treating stakeholders fairly** – asset management firms should think about how they treat their investors and their employees. Does the firm provide "psychological safety" for employees to speak out about bullying or for whistleblowing?

   - **Managing conflicts of interest** – Managing situations with potential conflicts of interest well is another way a firm can express its commitment to fairness.

- **Structuring remuneration** – Compensation is an important way a firm communicates fairness. It can be a good idea to sense-check employee compensation, to determine if there are ways in which it may inadvertently cause employee behaviors to be in conflict with the principle of fairness.

2. **Transparency** - "Honesty and openness" with which anyone who is representing a firm conducts themselves. Examples:

   - **Communicating with investors** – Today, investors seeking to place money with a firm demand a range of documentation, including compliance policies, information technology (IT), security information and regulatory filings. To be competitive, firms need to be consciously *transparent* in these areas.

   - **Engaging with employees** – Encouraging a culture of transparency – by maintaining clear and open lines of communication and encouraging a more collaborative working environment promotes operational efficiency. A good culture of openness and honesty can also help reduce risk and improve internal audit outcomes.

   - **Working with regulators** – A culture of openness and honesty helps build trust in relationships with regulators. Late or incorrect regulatory filings do considerable harm to this relationship. In short, for firms to thrive, they must understand the importance of communicating openly and honestly across their range of stakeholders, to build trust and deepen relationship.

3. **Diversity** – creating working environments that foster diversity of all kinds. Today firms are more diverse than they have ever been, as leadership realizes that an open approach to recruitment can supply important talent. In many ways, the financial services industry is moving towards a fairly successful meritocracy – those with talent, no matter where they hail from, have an opportunity to rise to the top.

In this article, Naughton holds that a culture of compliance sets the basis of behavior, integrity and accountability across an organization. This in turn fosters employee and client trust and confidence.

Using the same model above, let's look at compliance in a Church atmosphere. Can you see the three core values (Fairness, Transparency, and Diversity) operating within your Church? A culture of compliance impacts the way new members assimilate into the Church and how long they stay!

Compliance in a Church Setting

Most Churches have written standards or guidelines of some sort. Whether they are called By-laws, Constitution, Manuals, Preamble, or Standard Operating Procedures, its purpose is to establish structure or procedures for managing the Church. It should describe how the Church is organized and governed. Regarding the core value of **fairness** in the Church, if a survey was taken in your Church, what would the results yield? Would the majority of members say members are treated fairly and that "rules" apply to all? Would members feel there is a discrepancy between members who get a 'pass' and members who have to suffer the consequence? Would they say there is preferential treatment of some over others? This may all sound petty in nature; However small matters unhandled can result in great problems which affect the culture and morale of the Church. Handle a matter while it is small, and it won't get big! The Hebrew idiom (kal va-chomer) implies to take care of a problem while it is simple, and it won't become complex. Rather, "nip it in the bud."

In Paul's day, the Hellenistic Jews complained against the Hebraic Jews because their widows were being overlooked in the daily distribution of food (Acts 6:1). They complained they were not being treated fairly in the Church. The issue of members being treated unfairly is "nothing new under the sun." Paul had to set the Church in order regarding unfair treatment that existed in the Church.

Think about how you treat members of the Church. Look within and do an honest self-assessment. Do you treat every member in your church as your neighbor whom you love? Do you extend the same level of love and respect to members regardless of their status or role in the Church?

Is there a forum for resolving conflicts in your Church? Do members have an opportunity to present their concern before a forum? Do you find that most conflicts are minimized and regarded as unimportant? What about remuneration? Are members compensated the same? Are they compensated at all? The answer to these questions will allow you to determine if *your* Church is exercising the core value of **fairness** in promoting a culture of compliance.

Let's talk about the second core value of **transparency** in the Church-Honesty and Openness. Reflecting on my childhood years when I attended services at the local Roman Catholic Church, I can recall *some* Church statements being made publicly (to its members). In fact,

Church projects, a family's offerings, and monies collected from church social events such as Church bazaars were all public knowledge. Embarrassing as it may have been to families who did not make large (or any) contributions, it was still public knowledge. I recall also as an adult in the Church of God in Christ, that monies collected from Sunday School, general offerings and other auxiliaries were openly reported to the Church. Total amount of tithes and offerings collected was announced.

Naughton stresses the need for collaboration and maintaining clear and open lines of communication. Ask yourself, "Am I free to ask questions about the operation of the Church? Am I free to speak up in meetings without concerns for retaliation? Are there barriers to me speaking up?" A culture of openness and honesty helps to build trust between Leaders and members. In an environment where one is not free to speak without retribution, there will be a lack of trust in relationships and transparency will not exist. Churches require efficiency, as God is all efficient and a God of Order.

During the reign of King Joash over Judah, he decided to repair the Temple of Solomon, which had been damaged and sacred objects had been stolen from it (2 Chron. 24:7). All the officials and all the people brought their money *gladly*, dropping it into the chest made for its collections. The money was given to the men appointed to supervise the work on the Temple. With it they paid those who worked on the Temple of the Lord – the carpenters and builders, masons and stonecutters (2 Ki. 12:11-12).

> [15] *They did not require an accounting from those to whom they gave the money to pay the workers, because they acted with complete honesty (2 Ki. 12:15 NIV).*

Wow! Can you imagine appointing people to a project today, putting money in their hands and requiring no accountability? The money went from the Priest's hands, to the supervisor's hands, to the workers hands. The workers purchased the material needed and they did the work. I imagine today it would be a far-fetched idea! Living in the age of accountability where there is a need for Church audits, this process would not be feasible. Of greater concern is that of proven dishonesty and disloyalty in some Churches, coupled with scams and lawsuits. Again, this process would be non-existent. Perhaps King Joash and Jehoiada the Priest *knew* that the supervisors and workers could be trusted. In fact, there was money left over after the work was done, and they faithfully turned it in to the King and Priest!

> *14 When they had finished, they brought the rest of the money to the king and Jehoiada, and with it were made articles for the LORD's temple: articles for the service and for the burnt offerings, and also dishes and other objects of gold and silver (2 Chron. 24:14 NIV).*

Let us pray that the core value of transparency (honesty and openness) return to the house of God. It is necessary in order to build a culture of compliance.

Regarding the core value of **Diversity,** Churches still struggle in this 21st Century with recognizing one another's likenesses and respecting one another's differences. If we were all alike, what a boring world it would be! However, God allows us to enjoy a world of differences, choices, and variety! We struggle with fellowshipping, one church with another, because it's not "our way." We may love the foot-stomping, dancing, and loud music (because we believe heaven is loud), so we're uncomfortable in quiet settings where the people are encouraged to listen and learn quietly. OR, because our environment is so quiet, we reject the ones who prefer musical instruments and rejoicing because "they're too loud."

What about this one: we don't worship together because we're a Black church and they're a White church, or, they're a Hispanic church. Sadly, Church programs are geared to the 'culture of the church' rather than to God's agenda. We are afraid of diversity and have become judgmental on how others feel led to praise God. So, we rob ourselves of the beauty of diversity. We fail to embrace and respect different cultures and the gifts and talents they possess. We do perish for lack of knowledge! We remain ignorant of others' ways of reaching the same God, the God of Abraham, Isaac and Jacob (for clarity). I do believe He basks in the diversity of praise and worship that ascends to the heavens.

In Dr. Tony Evans' book, *Let's Get to Know Each Other*: *What White Christians Should Know About Black Christians* (1995), Dr. Evans shares his testimony:

> "As we enter the 21st Century, this problem (Biblical mandate for Unity) continues to plague us. It was in 1969 I was told by the Leadership of a large Southern Baptist Church in Atlanta that I wasn't welcome there. It was in 1974 that my wife and I were informed in no uncertain terms that we were not welcome in a prominent Bible Church in Dallas, pastored by the way, by one of my seminary professors. It was in 1987 that I was told by a number of major Christian radio station managers that there was little place for Blacks in the general Christian broadcast media. And it was in 1993 that I heard a major influential national Christian leader say that, based on the curse of Ham, black people are under God's judgement. Today I regularly get calls from church leaders across the

country, both blacks and whites, telling me of the racial tensions in their community and division among their churches. Our Ministry, The Urban Alternative, is called upon to work with individual churches as well as groups of churches on how to help them address the lack of unity, which not only exists in the society at large, but continuously plagues the Body of Christ" (Chap 7, pgs. 117-118).

He wrote this book in 1995. Sadly, in 2020 the lack of unity, coupled with the problem of racism, still plagues society and the Body of Christ. In her book, *Martyrs for the Movement: Black Bodies, Civil Rights and #BlackLivesMatter,* Dr. Dorinda Rolle addresses the connection between past and current events related to social justice, especially with regard to issues that affect the African American community. The anthology delves into the devaluing of black people's personhood and agency. It challenges readers to think critically and spark dialogue about race in America. Dr. Rolle is an adjunct professor of African American studies at the University of Texas at San Antonio.

I'm convinced that Heaven is not all Black, or all White, or all Latino, or all Asian. So, we'd better get used to each other down here on earth, because in Heaven, we're all one! If we don't have the three core values (fairness, transparency, diversity), a culture of compliance will not exist. A church culture of compliance calls for all of us to dwell together in unity.

Psalm 133

Behold, how good and how pleasant it is For brothers to dwell together in unity! [2] It is like the precious oil upon the head, Coming down upon the beard,

Even Aaron's beard,
Coming down upon the edge of his robes.
³ It is like the dew of Hermon
Coming down upon the mountains of Zion;
*For **there** the LORD commanded the blessing—*
life for evermore.

For **there** (in unity) comes His blessing. What happens in unity? Answer: The Lord commands the blessing! Could the lack of unity cause blessings not to flow? I think the answer to be a resounding "Yes!"

After the death of Solomon, Israel went through a tumultuous time and the Kingdom was divided. Jeroboam became King over 10 tribes in the North (Israel), and Rehoboam (son of Solomon) was King over two tribes in the South (Judah) (1 Ki. 12). Israel went through a succession of evil Kings who perpetuated a culture of non-compliance with God's laws and continued to engage in idolatry. Ahab was the worst, urged by his wife Jezebel (I Ki. 21:21). Elijah the prophet comes on the scene and challenges the people:

> *"How long will you waver between two opinions? If the LORD is God, follow him; but if Baal is God, follow him." But the people said nothing (1 Ki. 18:21 NIV).*

A church whereby *the people say nothing* in regard to injustices, unfair treatment of others, or teachings or practices not commensurate with the Word of God will **never** generate a culture of compliance with the laws of God. They will continue with the "status quo" (existing state) and will fail to thrive as God intended. We're commanded in Scripture to "*Speak up for those who cannot speak for* *themselves, for the rights of all who are destitute. Speak up and judge fairly; defend the rights of the poor and needy" (Pr. 31:8-9 NIV).*

Exercising the three core values of **fairness, transparency and diversity** will help to generate a culture of compliance within our Churches. We are charged individually to grow in Christian virtue and to walk in love. The Apostle Peter admonishes us to add to our faith moral excellence, knowledge, self-control, perseverance, godliness, brotherly kindness, love and says "…*for as long as you practice these things, you will never stumble" (2 Pet. 1: 5-10).*

Likewise, when Jesus was asked what is the greatest commandment He replied, *"Love the Lord your God with all your heart and with all your soul and with all your mind. This is the first and greatest; and the second is like it: Love your neighbor as yourself. All the Law and the prophets hang on these two commandments" (Matt. 22:36-40).* A culture of compliance promotes love from a pure heart, a good conscience and a sincere faith *(1 Tim. 1:8).* Love covers ALL of the commandments! When we truly walk in love, we are in compliance with the commandments, precepts, statutes and laws of God.

What then does a Culture of Compliance look like? The answer is, one that adheres to the Word of God, one that teaches sound doctrine, one that stimulates one another to love and good deeds, and one that encourages one another according to Heb. 10:24. Compliance in the Church is one that promotes the laws of God above the church or man-made laws and agendas, and is transformed into one where God is glorified in true worship:

> *The time is coming indeed and is here now – when true worshipers will worship the Father in spirit and in truth. The Father is looking for those who will worship Him that way (John 4:23).*

A Culture of Compliance looks like *Eph. 5:1-2*

> *Therefore, be imitators of God, as beloved children;*
> *[2] and walk in love, just as Christ also loved you and*
> *gave Himself up for us, an offering and a sacrifice to*
> *God as a fragrant aroma.*

When the Church is able to follow this classic example, it is then and only then that a **culture of compliance** can be fully embraced.

REFERENCES

Enduring Word Bible Commentary on Acts 20, David Guzik, 2006.

Evans, Tony. *Let's Get to Know Each Other: What White Christians Should Know About Black Christians.* Thomas Nelson Publishers, 1995.

Hahn, Thich Nhat. *The Art of Communicating.* Harper Collins Publishers, 2013.

Jastrao, Morris Jr, et al. *JewishEncyclopedia. com>5254>* (Zeb 54b). *Doeg.* KTAV Publishing House, 1960.

Kent, William. "Indulgences." The Catholic Encyclopedia. Vol. 7. New York: Robert Appleton Company, 1910. 14 Jun 2020. http://www. newadvent. org/cathen/07783a. htm.

Longree, Karla, and Gertrude Armbruster. *Quantity Food Sanitation, Fifth Edition.* John Wiley & Sons, 1996.

Mastery Technologies, Inc. *5 Elements of Effective Communication.* BBB Business Review, 2020. http://masterytcn. com n. d.,

Matthew Henry Commentary Concise, London: Hodder & Stoughton, 1706, 1995.

Naughton, Philip. *Compliance Culture: Building an Approach on Three Core Values,* Blog Post, FinExtra. 31 August 2018,

Risser, John D. *Know Them Which Labor Among You, Berean* Ministry 2018, (https://www. bereanvoice. org)

Rolle, Dorinda. *Martyrs for the Movement: Black Bodies, Civil Rights and #BlackLivesMatter.* Cognella Academic Publishing, 2020.

REFERNCES

Stone, Lawrence J, and Church, Joseph. *Child and Adolescence:* A *Psychology of the Growing Person*, *3rd Edition,* Random House, New York, 1973.

The Wycliffe Bible Commentary, Moody Press, Chicago, 1990.

Ethel Morale Gathers

As Chapter President of Dedicated Women in Christ (DWIC) Ministries, San Antonio, Texas, Ethel Gathers is a devoted Mother, Mentor, Teacher and Preacher of God's Word.

Her gift of teaching and ministering the Word of God was first recognized in the Church of God in Christ where she was called to ministry and licensed in 1982. Having served in the Military twenty years, her calling of teaching and preaching God's Word was recognized abroad. While stationed 5 years in Germany, she served as a Lay-Leader within the Chaplain services, where she ministered to countless members in Europe. Returning stateside in 1988, she was recognized as a Minister and ordained as an Elder in 1989 at her local Church, New Life Christian Center, San Antonio, TX. Her gift of teaching continued in her service as Sunday School teacher and Instructor at the New Life Living Word Seminary, where she helped prepare others for Ministerial licensure. As part of the Jail Ministry, Elder Gathers ministered to countless persons who were incarcerated and was instrumental in winning souls to Christ. She is a sought-after speaker in local churches and a conference speaker across denominations. She continues to minister to small groups such as troubled teens and post substance-abuse offenders.

An avid student of the educational system, Ethel Gathers holds a Doctorate in Religious Education from Bible Believers Christian College & Seminary, Los Angeles, CA.; a Master of Education Degree with a concentration in Counseling from Boston University, a certified Guidance Counselor License in the Commonwealth of Massachusetts, and a Master of Arts Degree in Theology from St. Mary's University, San Antonio, TX. She is a Certified Restorative Therapist through the Faith-Based Counselor Training Institute (FBCTI), State of Texas.

Ethel Gathers is a proud Veteran who served 11 years in the United States Air Force and 12 years in the United States Army. Discharged honorably with high achievements, her services to her country continued as a civil service worker, Lackland Air Force Base, San Antonio, TX, culminating in a recent retirement.

She is the proud mother of 4 daughters: Nathasha, Chastity, LeKeisha and Alaina, Grandmother to thirteen grandchildren who affectionately call her "Honey," and was blessed recently with a beautiful great-grandchild, Aaliyah Joi, who brings the family much "Joi."

DEDICATED WOMEN IN CHRIST (DWIC) MINISTRY
San Antonio Chapter

Ethel Gathers, President
Cell: (210) 618-7107; egathers@att.net

Mary Wooldridge, Vice President
(210) 445-9539; marywooldridge@att.net

A Ministry given in prayer, to a small group of women in Landstuhl, Germany, 1986.

DWIC expanded to Four Chapters in the United States with Headquarters in Las Vegas, NV, and subsequent Chapters in Pensacola, FL., Oxford, MS. and San Antonio, TX.

Mission Statement: Women dedicated to loving, encouraging, and building each other in Christ by caring, sharing, and reaching out to others in Love.

Tools of this Ministry include: Workshops, Seminars, Conferences, Retreats and Outreach.

** Elder Gathers is a sought-after Speaker who ministers to all age groups**

www.ethelgathers.carrd.co

ENDORSEMENTS

CHURCH CULTURE: WHAT MEMBERS DARE NOT SAY

"In her book *Church Culture: What Members Dare Not Say,* the author spells out the primary purpose of ministry and the responsibilities of both, church leaders and church members. Her brilliant, well crafted, powerful, and thought-provoking questions serve as a guide to ascertain which direction "your" church is moving —one that uplifts the Word of God, or one that leads to failure. A must read for all churches, large or small, regardless of denomination."

Joyce Robertson
Author of *Like Dad Use to Say*
And
The Biography of a Woman who Did it All

"**Liberating** is the word that best describes Ethel Gathers' book, *Church Culture*: *What Members Dare Not Say.* When unscriptural conduct is sanctioned from the pulpit, church members tend to suffer in silence.

Church Culture: What Members Dare Not Say, gives the reader three things: 1. understanding of the wrongs going on inside some of our churches, 2. a true scriptural basis for each situation, and 3. the power to say, "No more!" It is well-written, compassionate, and scripturally based. Whether you're the abuser or the victim, this book is for you. *What Members Dare Not Say* pours light on a very dark subject and will bring healing to many."

Anita M. McLaurin
Children's Book Author
My Father Said I Could

"Outside of the Word of God and the workings of the Holy Spirit, church culture is one of the most powerful forces operating within the church. It has the power to shape the Church into all of those things Christ said we should and could be, as well as the power to be used by the enemy to tear down and destroy. This book is well-written noting the writer's experiences, and commentary supported by skillful scrutiny of scripture that puts *what members dare not say* into perspective. The book highlights how leaders and believers in the Body of Christ can do better until we all come into the unity of the faith."

Dorinda Rolle, PhD
Author
Martyrs for the Movement: Black bodies, Civil Rights and
#BlackLivesMatter

What a powerful message to Church leaders on accountability in this book *"Church Culture: What Members Dare Not Say.* When an atmosphere is created that DOES NOT enable the spiritual needs of the body of Christ to be met, the spirit of God will be hindered. The message to the controlling leaders and members for the church is to return to being the spiritual cornerstone of the community minus the layers of infrastructure that create division. More than ever, the church's role is to be a sacred place that offers comfort, spiritual stability and endorses obedience to his commands and statutes!

Mary Wooldridge
Author of *Recipe for FORGIVENESS: A Choice Delight for a Richer Life!*

Heavenly Realm Publishing

Heavenly Realm Publishing is dedicated to ensuring that we take care of all of our authors/customers, and that their publishing and printing needs are met and exceeded. We offer high-quality publishing, printing, video, CD & DVD printing, portrait studio/digital printing, design websites and hosting and design services, and a retail online outlet. We are committed to providing you with top notch Author Advising support at no cost. All of our authors are orientated to understand the publishing and printing process.

We serve a wide range of authors/customers worldwide, and value every author's/customer's relationship greatly. Each service we offer benefits from the depth and breadth of our expertise. We approach every author/customer with a focus on integrity, advocacy, and understanding. We enhance your book, video, and photo vision, you keep all of the rights and rewards.

www.ingramcontent.com/pod-product-compliance
Lightning Source LLC
Chambersburg PA
CBHW071052090426

42737CB00013B/2335

9781944383206